THE BEST IN

SCIENCE, OFFICE AND
BUSINESS PARK
DESIGN

THE BEST IN

SCIENCE, OFFICE AND

BUSINESS PARK

DESIGN

ALAN PHILLIPS

B.T. Batsford Ltd • London

A QUARTO BOOK

Published by B. T. Batsford Ltd
4 Fitzhardinge Street
London W1H 0AH

ISBN 0-7134-7397-5

This book was designed and produced by
Quarto Publishing plc
6 Blundell Street
London N7 9BH

Creative Director: Richard Dewing
Designer: Chris Dymond
Editor: Viv Croot
Picture Researcher: Jan Croot

Typeset in Great Britain by
Central Southern Typesetters, Eastbourne
Manufactured in Hong Kong by Regent Publishing Services Limited
Printed in Hong Kong by Leefung-Asco Printers Ltd

Contents

Introduction 6

The First Generation: Business Park Progenitors 26

The Second Generation: Business and the Community 70

The Third Generation: Developing the Neighbourhood 100

The Fourth Generation: The New Villages 166

The Park Idea: Variations on a Theme 206

Index of Projects 222

Directory of Practising Architects 223

Photographic Acknowledgements 224

Introduction

There is an implicit contradiction in the term *business park*. A park is a place, generally within a town or city, reserved for sports, leisure and pleasure. Business is associated with transaction, concentrated effort and commerce. However, the prevailing ethos of the development institutions which are currently building business parks means that this oxymoron is resolved through a total integration of work and recreation: well-crafted buildings dedicated to prestige technology-based corporations are set within a man-made landscape that provides the visual and interactive amenities of a rural environment, as well as the facility of automobile access to the front door of the office. The contemporary business

park seeks to homogenize productivity requirements, employer and employee aspirations and high technology corporate image with good architecture, the immediate landscape and the holistic development master plan. To achieve this requires a complex and committed effort on behalf of a huge team of experts, including developers, economists, architects, engineers, landscape architects, planners, public relations agencies, marketing companies and tenants. In addition, there is a schedule of criteria that needs to be satisfied if all these skills are to be brought together for the overall benefit of the developer, the business park community and the community at large.

Birmingham Business Park

The ideal of the business park is to integrate the
workplace in a carefully arranged rural setting, taking
quality of life into the equation when balancing
employee and employer inspirations. Birmingham
Business Park is a third generation park, with a floorplate
to open space ratio of 25% to 30%, where the park is
larger than the business.

Context Perhaps the most critical decision in business park development is the site. A good park will be located by a freeway, or preferably at the intersection of two or more. The development will be close to a large conurbation or metropolitan district with an established downtown trading centre, and be linked by rapid public transport systems. For overseas trade, the site will be close to an international airport, or support a local airport with a one-stop international connection. The site will also need to connect, reinforce and enhance the indigenous community, whereby a planning transaction can take place between the amenities of the new development and the services of existing infrastructures. The geography, geology and morphology of the site should be such that the development provides a considerable improvement in the visual amenity of the area, notwithstanding the introduction of buildings to a location that was previously rural and undeveloped.

Also linked to the issues of context is the economic equation. Just as a partnership exists between the new development and its contribution to the increased value of its local environment, so a formula has to be established between the price of the site and the ability to afford the proper quality of development. Because a previous criteria for site selection depends on the degree by which the area may be improved by development, it follows that the existing site has a low intrinsic value and can be purchased within the terms of the economic equation. The balance needed to be established within the tripod of *quality, cost* and *value* will play as large a part in the preferred context of a business park as any other condition prevailing upon the selection of a suitable site for commercial development within a rural or suburban location.

Stockley Park: Before

Looking like an iron age fort, the raw bones of Stockley Park show the underlying landscaping of the site.

Stockley Park: After

The end product shows the realization of the idea, good architecture well placed in a maturing landscape.

STOCKLEY PARK
LANDSCAPE MASTER PLAN
0 25 50   100m

Stockley Park Landscape Master Plan

An optimum relationship between the scale of
development and the area of open space provides for
business and pleasure to coexist without contradiction.

Scale Business parks require substantial areas of land to guarantee their
success. If the relationship between price of land and its quality of
development is inversely proportional, then a direct relationship exists between
the size of a development and its quality.

Beyond building a *park*, with the traditional constituent elements of
greenlands, waterways, walkways, lakes and planted landscaping, the
business park must integrate secondary and tertiary highways, a servicing
matrix of utilities, high density car parking and the buildings themselves. To
achieve a result in which the park element is dominant enough to sustain its
own definition in terms of non-developable open space, and also contain
enough buildings to support the central amenity facilities that create a sense of
an integrated community, the development site must achieve a *critical mass*.

A làrge site not only allows for the development to be planned and designed
as a recognizable *place* in its own right, but has the advantage of becoming
flexible enough for various areas of the development to be conceived as
neighbourhoods, having a design that simultaneously integrates itself with its
domestic context, as well as having an architectural specificity to urban or rural
phenomena that happen to influence one boundary area of the site, but not
another. The smaller the park, the more likely it is to be overcome by its
environs, and the less likely to afford amenities .

Density The optimum critical mass achieved, a business park development will next look to the issues of density. Planning authorities, development agencies and marketing consultants will all have views on the ratio of car parking to building development population, the area of building floorplate to gross acre, and the preferred height of building, all of which should generally allow for 40 per cent of off-plot amenity landscape to secure the conditions implicit in the reconciliation of scale and context to financial feasibility. Many parks are designed against a yardstick of 10,000 sq ft of building floorplate per gross acre, with parking for every employee. These two criteria combine to determine the road system, utility infrastructure and ratios between open space building mass and hard landscape and, if well designed, can prove a satisfactory equation. But if the idea of community is to be preserved, densities should vary throughout the park, in order to avoid monotony and to establish quarters or neighbourhoods that are referential to recognized paradigms and precedents. As business parks grow to such a size that they can be compared to villages or small towns, then successful urban figures like the village green, town square or civic plaza can be used as models to justify higher or lower *regional* densities in the cause of composition and development topography.

Stockley Park

Arup Associates development at 1 Long Walk Road clusters buildings at the entrance of Stockley Park, overlooking the Arena lake and the golf course, at once uniting work, rest and play.

The Master Plan

If context, scale and density are the criteria against which the feasibility of a business park can be judged, the master plan is the instrument of planning and implementation. Beyond the economics and mathematics of land acquisition, plot ratios, infrastructural utility mechanics and highway engineering, the master plan provides the principal act of design. But rather than a general statement of intent, perhaps no more than lotting up the site beyond the design and building of the road and utility systems, a master plan must be quite precise in the shape, arrangement and zoning of individual buildings within their boundaries and among their neighbourhoods in order to bring clarity and homogeneity to the whole, while leaving flexibility for individual statements of architectural expression. The master plan will seek to promote control *and* choice, within a hard and soft landscaped framework, that is formal enough to characterize the site and informal enough to establish the *genius loci*.

The master plan is also a proving and protecting tool. It will enable prospective tenants to see that the principal benefit of parking-at-the-front-door can be realized, and that aspect, prospect and orientation, no matter who designs the individual building, can be achieved inside the plot boundary and within the neighbourhood matrix. It will protect the indigenous ecologies of the site including, for example, woodlands and wetlands, and provide systems of land drainage balancing lakes to encourage wildlife. For the physical population, the master plan will provide for security systems, and a central amenity complex comprising shops, banks, gyms, bars and managerial suites, as well as pathways for internal pedestrian use.

Finally, as well as being an environmental policeman, the master plan also provides for the careful democratization of the site. Public rights of way are protected and enhanced, and new walks are created as discrete circulation spaces from the distributor roads, that allow the public to enjoy the park and its amenities while not intruding on the necessarily more private realms of research buildings or computer facilities. Consequently, the master plan will provide for soft landscape buffer zones that are benign to the needs of all, without the requirements for the ubiquitous boundary fence, or threatening sentry post. Lastly, the master plan will provide standards for clear but discreet signage of the site and the overall control of graphics, street furniture, bus and rail stop points that, when badly considered, so often compromise a park's visual quality.

The Carnegie Center

Graphics, signage and street furniture are considered at the master plan stage.

Marina Village

One of the principal skills of masterplanning is to design
an holistic development structure that allows for both
control and choice.

Occupation and Preservation A park will only be as good as the people who use it, and the people who run it. During the early period of business park development, when the word 'park' referred to the attitude of a stationary car rather than the green lung of a townscape, the architecture was often as poor as the landscape, with buildings for component manufacturers and equipment assemblers only one step away from the industrial or trading estate. Parks have developed to become an appropriate environment for high-profile, high-technology corporations who seek to declare a prestige product by association with good architecture, good art and a good landscape design. Rather than scarring the park with open storage areas, poor environmental auditing and erratic maintenance programs, the tenant and landlord work in close partnership to maintain the highest standards of building design, ecology and preservation. Contemporary management analysts support the view that there is a strong connection between productivity and the quality of the workplace. Compared with the inner city, with its problems of transport, pollution, violence and poor health, the business park is seen not as a type of light industrial suburb laying around the outskirts of mass housing schemes, but as a clean '*village*' complex that is easy to get to, pleasant to stay in and comfortable to leave. Because the population is fixed by permanent standards of density and plot ratios, there are no queues in and no queues out. Roads are big enough, bars are not too busy and the bank is a lakeside walk away. For these reasons, and because a high investment environment can generally only be afforded by wealthy multi-national corporations, the business park has developed into an arcadia of lunchtime picnics, workouts in the gyms, and birthday parties in the local wine bar overlooking snow-white swans and koi carp the size of dolphins.

Although management maintain a duty to keep public ways clean, landscape tidy and all the provisions of the master plan in place, it is usually with the cooperation of the tenant. More essentially, the on-site management team concentrate on the legal structure of the park. Because of a mutual ambition to enhance the environment, covenants are generally protective rather than restrictive.

Contemporary business park management policies are becoming more flexible, with owner-occupiers profiting from freeholdings and investors owning freeholds with leasehold occupiers.

Stockley Park Arena
Restaurant

A fixed population generally ensures that amenities can
be designed to an optimum brief.

Evolution The sophistication of today's multi-neighbourhood, amenity-resourced business park evolved from topographical phenomena and planning legislation. Many cities throughout the world came about not by the product of a grand plan, but by the gradual growth and subsequent fusion of previously independent settlements.

Fragments of the open land that separated the settlements or villages were saved to become *commons, greens* or *parks*, while rapid and often random development subsumed the indigenous topology to create large metropolitan districts and everlasting holistic city units. While commerce, banking and government identified a typical downtown district, light industry was often left to occupy those parts left over, as the pattern of inner city development broke down around what became the inner ring road. Although transport systems were good, land was environmentally poor, which led to cheap land price, even cheaper industrial sheds, and the advent of the trading *estate*. As inner city real estate values increased, residential districts were bought out by expanding commercial and shopping sectors, with a displaced population encouraged to migrate to what is now known as suburbia.

As housing developments with large gardens, public open spaces and intimate shopping precincts rubbed shoulders with established but discrete light industries, community, work and leisure came almost naturally to coalesce. The growth of villages and towns into cities inevitably introduces *rus*

Radburn, New Jersey

Built in 1928, Radburn was planned to take into account the consequences of mass car ownership, and the problem of parking.

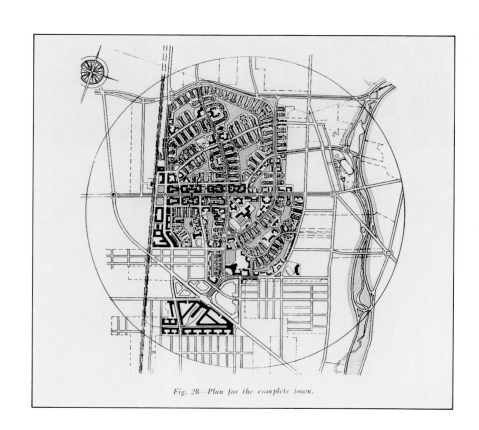

Fig. 28—Plan for the complete town.

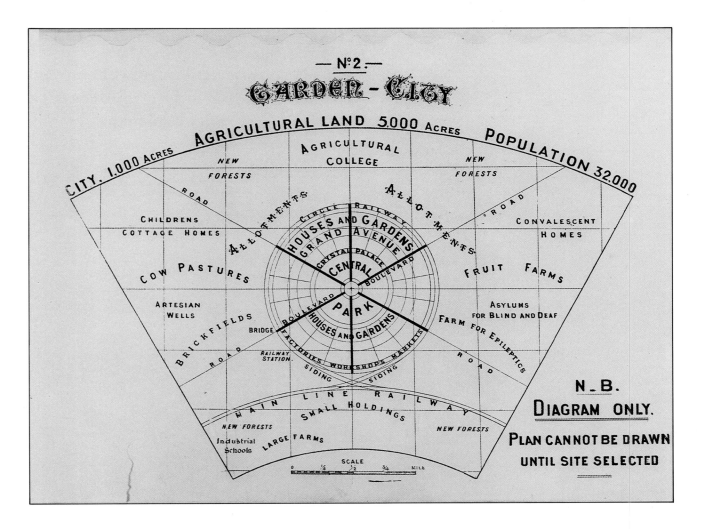

Garden City, Letchworth

In 1898, Ebenezer Howard, a City of London clerk, proposed the idea of the Garden City, which would combine the dynamics of the city with the spaciousness of the countryside in a logically developed setting. Howard considered the optimum population of such a city to be 32,000 people, and the railway to be its principal transport nexus. The Garden City at Letchworth (above) was developed by Howard with the architects and planners Parker and Unwin.

in urbe (the country in the town) and *urbs in rure* (the town in the country), providing an historical precedent for the arcadian concept of the English Garden City promoted by architects and planners Parker and Unwin at Letchworth in 1903. Their own weaving workshop at Saint Edmundsbury was a testimonial to the ability of electric power to have industry clothed in a manner that was benign to houses, shops and offices, to become, perhaps, the earliest example of a single use business park, although fully integrated into the vision of a garden city.

The appeal of community living, working and leisure within an *urbs-in-rure* environment grew through the 1920s and 1930s. Large concentrations of people, industry and wealth had politicians in Europe and the United States concerned about the social and economic balance of their nation. Legislation that promised cheap development land promulgated a model British industrial estate at Team Valley in Gateshead, Tyne and Wear.

With developing problems of car transport, planners referred to the 1928 Radburn development in New Jersey as a garden city proposal that confronted the issue of mass car ownership. At Radburn, cars were directred to the edge of the site with housing 'super blocks' turning their backs to the road to face areas of pedestrianized open space. This housing paradigm was used in the British Teeside industrial estate of 1964, which confirmed the early American conclusion, now common to all business parks, that a high-profile frontage was no longer an *a priori* requirement for commercial development. As car pollution became worse during the 1960s, agencies such as the Location of

Offices Bureau encouraged new office developments away from downtown areas. This move, together with the success of many industrial estates and an almost innate sense of wanting to live and work in a garden city environment, influenced the planning of many greenfield university developments and university-led science and research parks. During the 1970s, the experience was fed back to new town development corporations. The business district was planned as separate from downtown, set in a 'park', communalized, landscaped and car-parked. Downtown daytime populations and traffic congestion was relieved, to make way for the pedestrianized shopping

Birmingham Business Park

There is a strong eighteenth- and nineteenth-century resonance in many business parks. Carefully placed lakes, meandering waterways, cunningly sited vistas and nodding groves of symmetrical trees all pay homage to such landscape architects as Capability Brown and Humphrey Repton, the tireless improvers of many great English estates.

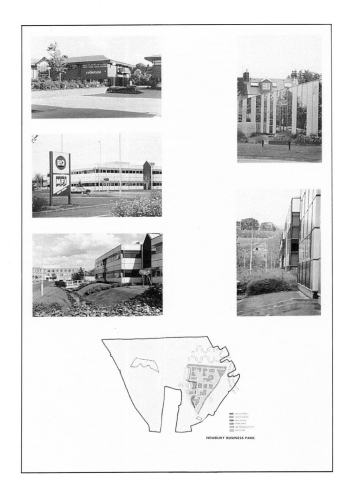

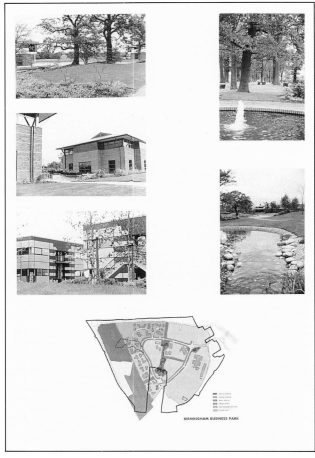

Masterplanning

Business park development involves an enormous
amount of co-ordination between architects, landscape
architects, engineers, developers, local authorities,
transport regulation bodies and clients. Such co-
ordination is one function of the masterplanner. The
Master Plan files for some of the projects developed by
Arlington Properties of England are shown above.

precincts, banking, insurance, theatre and administration districts that could
be served by low-cost public rapid transport systems.

Although ideal in concept, the first generation business park did little more
than install a road and utilities infrastructure, lot-up the site, landscape the
leftovers and sell off. Sites were too small to sustain amenity and community
facilities, leaving employees isolated.

As business parks developed, it became clear that sizes would have to
increase in order to achieve the critical mass required to afford the supporting
facilities of shops and recreation. Although many of the criteria for a 'true
business park' were satisfied in the second generation series, standardized and
uniform plot densities tended towards the 'protective cage' approach to
landscaping, which led to a series of unrelated buildings of approximately
equivalent size, screened within a large dominating landscape, leaving few
opportunities for the creation of groupings and a consequential hierarchy of
spatial, architectural and landscaping neighbourhoods.

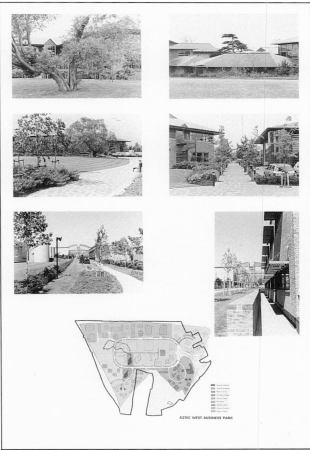

It is the development of scale, hierarchy and grouping that distinguish a third generation park from its progenitors. The master planning principles embrace the same theories that would comprise the infrastructure of a small new town, of which first generation parks were once a part, with the scale of development increasing from 40 acres to two or three hundred. The central amenity building has become an identifiable place, or miniature 'downtown', to support groups of neighbourhoods that vary in density and plot size to establish a variety of districts for a variety of occupiers, within an holistic park concept.

It is inevitable that a fourth and final generation will appear. This will be something like a business village that, by introducing housing and education, will establish an entirely autonomous development that can turn its back on the city from which it evolved to create a form that is totally divorced from the planning influences of *suburbanitas*, to become a new architectural paradigm and development typology.

A loss for the city or a gain for the

country? The organic structure of a city is too complex for its analysis to form part of this introduction. And yet the intrigue and success of city life is that within one large metropolitan area, the desire for variety *and* constancy is sustained by the city's ability to accept change and reinforce permanency. The city is like a huge cultural barometer that records the mood of change and responds by successive regeneration. Great monuments like cathedrals, palaces and museums sustain the comfort of constancy and, with urban housing and city squares, are restored and preserved. Against this matrix, other buildings die and are torn down to give way to new cinemas, schools, hospitals, parks and offices. The commercial sector has always been at the heart of a city. Trade is its lifeblood. If the world's city transport systems ultimately fail, and the giants of industry abandon downtown for the playing fields of rural arcadia, to replace the messenger and board room with video, fax and tele-conferencing; and if the huge population of suburbians find themselves with a ten-minutes drive to park outside lakeside office windows, there will be left either the commercial morgue of a lifeless urban ghetto, or the greatest inner city redevelopment opportunity of the century.

Newbury Business Park

One of the delightful by-products of business park landscaping has been the rapid colonization of woods and water by a wide variety of wildlife, attracted by unpolluted habitats and a generous food supply.

The First Generation: Business Park Progenitors

The modern business park evolved from a building type more commonly known as the industrial estate. Often sited on the edge of an existing town, or adjacent to the suburbs of a small city, the estate comprised small groups of buildings, usually dedicated to light industrial, warehouse or component businesses.

Sites were either lotted up and sold off with a build permit to the incoming tenant, or pre-developed by the owner to be leased out. But generally, the standard of architecture was low, with a proliferation of access roads, hardstandings and open storage units, and an almost complete absence of landscaping. And yet they did continue the idea of community working that had become popular, especially in British and American cities, by the enthusiasm of planners and the encouragement of federal land legislation. The first generation 'parks' are still being constructed to cater particularly for those businesses that are industrially based rather than research or commercially orientated. Although

the scale of development is often too modest to afford the quality of environment and support facilities of the second and third generation parks, the general standard of architecture has improved to a degree so that even the most ordinary of sheds declares a concern for excellence, whether in the structural detailing, hard landscape design or graphics.

Although there are rarely opportunities affordable for place-making, the Grianan Centre at Dundee Technology Park in Scotland demonstrates how a speculative brief for a first generation park can celebrate the *genius loci* of a site, even to the point of exposing the geomorphology to become part of the architectonic intervention.

In central London, the Bricklayers Arms development establishes frames in space and site markers as two of many devices that serve to raise what might have been an ordinary *no-architecture* project to a skilful and elegant place-making composition that frames an architecture of delightful irony.

South Newmoor

LOCATION: Irvine, Ayrshire, Scotland

NAME OF PROJECT: South Newmoor Phase 8

SIZE: Three units at 1,000m^2

FUNCTION OF BUILDING: Speculative low-cost factory space

DATE OF COMPLETION: February 1991

ARCHITECT: Irvine Development Corporation. Chief Architect/Planner: Ian Downs; Project Architect: Roan Rutherford

This project was designed to meet the need for speculative, low-cost factories. The planning brief was for the factories to be black and/or white. The factory was designed all white for two reasons. The first being the practical reason that all the low cost components were available in white as a standard finish. The second being that white would help to articulate the detailing of the components on which the design depended. The design is a simple square pyramid with boilers mounted on a crow's nest on the central column.

The building is surrounded with a canopy to give weather protection in one of the wettest areas of Britain. It also gives shade in summer, while allowing sunlight penetration from a low winter sun. The detailing of the canopy is designed to provide lightness and intricacy. The three buildings at Irvine in Scotland are good examples of carefully detailed pavilions. The clarity and elegance of these modest sheds is in sharp contrast to the surrounding landscape.

Hampshire International Park

LOCATION: Chineham, Basingstoke, Hampshire, England

NAME OF PROJECT: 'Tulips' Building for Centerprise International Ltd

SIZE: 7,000m²

FUNCTION OF BUILDING: Computer company factory/offices/warehouse

DATE OF COMPLETION: Ongoing

ARCHITECT: John Lyall Architects, London, England

'Tulips' was designed to be built and occupied in phases. There are sales offices, product demonstration areas, production and servicing areas, together with a very busy warehouse function. Therefore, there are distinct activities which occupy similarly-designed floor space either side of the central atrium which is three storeys high.

The Tulips building illustrates how good architecture can be quarried from a low budget brief to be subsequently abandoned in a field of mediocrity. However, the juxtaposition of modest elegance in an undeveloped landscape may well prove to be a more encouraging circumstance, especially if the park's tubular logo serves as a paradigm to future developments.

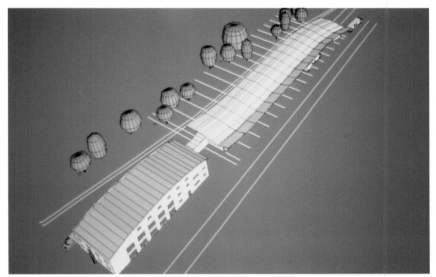

Tulips Phase 2: Aerial view

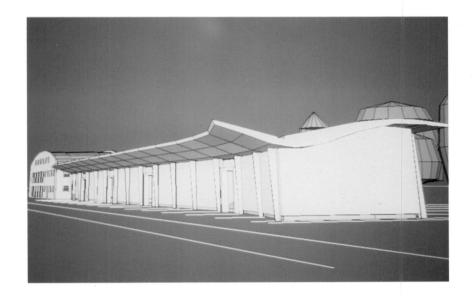

Chilworth

LOCATION: Chilworth, Southampton, England

NAME OF PROJECT: Chilworth Research Centre

SIZE: 30,000m²

FUNCTION OF BUILDING: Scientific research and development

DATE OF COMPLETION: 1990

ARCHITECT: Edward Cullinan, Mark Beedle, Roddy Langmuir, Mary-Lou Arscott/Cullinan, Architects, London, England

Sprung-loaded, timber-slatted vertical blinds poised at right angles to adjacent fenestration systems provide sun screens to the serialised, top-hung window system. The tertiary elements of fabric sitting lightly against a low cost wall, provide reflections to reinforce the dramatic aesthetic that can be achieved from simple repetition. The four buildings surrounding the central circus seem to poke their noses over the garden wall by way of reminding the observer that architecture and landscape work together as a place-making activity.

Chilworth Research Centre

continued over page

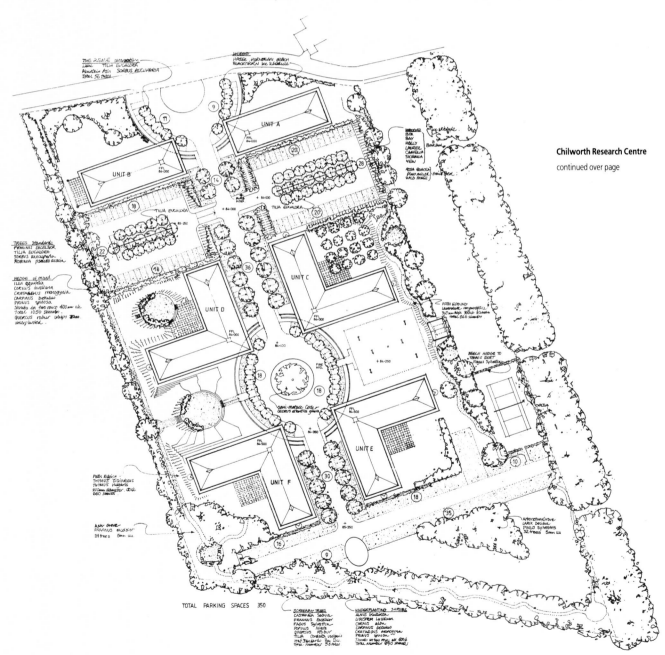

CHILWORTH PARK PHASE 2 · SITE PLAN

Chilworth Research Centre
continued

Only six buildings comprise Phase 2 of the Chilworth project, but their symmetrical arrangement about a primary avenue and oval circus secures a geometrical harmony within a modest landscape. The modest roof plan belies an elegantly detailed corner condition of richness and complexity.

Waterside Business Park

LOCATION: Witham, Essex, England

SIZE: 3.87 acres

FUNCTION OF BUILDING: Speculative business buildings

DATE OF COMPLETION: 1990

ARCHITECT: Robert Tear Architects, Southampton, Hampshire, England

Waterside is next to a green belt site, and is focused on a central pond. The pond is a balancing lagoon related to flooding problems and incorporates features which encourage the regeneration of a sympathetic natural environment.

Hayward Business Centre

LOCATION: Havant, Hampshire, England

SIZE: 3.28 acres

FUNCTION OF BUILDING: Speculative development for light industry

DATE OF COMPLETION: 1990

ARCHITECT: Robert Tear Architects, Southampton, Hampshire, England

Hayward Business Centre was developed in two phases. Phase I was finished in 1987.

Bishops Square

LOCATION: Hatfield, Hertfordshire, England

SIZE: 18,522m²

DATE OF COMPLETION: 1992

ARCHITECT: Scott, Brownrigg & Turner, Guildford, Surrey, England

Bishops Square is one of many examples of what could be termed the single cell park. Close to a city centre, a park has been quarried out of the existing urban fabric to provide a landscape, a single corporation. This type of development distinguishes itself from the conventional city office building to become appropriate within the building type category of business parks in that the building and its site go to create what is understood as an urban park.

Hampshire Corporate Park

LOCATION: Chandler's Ford, Hampshire, England

SIZE: 18 acres

NAME OF PROJECT: Unit 3

FUNCTION OF BUILDING: Speculative offices

DATE OF COMPLETION: Unit 3 completed 1986
(14,000m^2); overall completion 1988

ARCHITECT: HGP Greentree Allchurch Evans Ltd,
Fareham, Hampshire, England

The first units to be completed at the Hampshire Corporate Business Park are now framed by a maturing landscape. Intimate courtyards are characterized by carefully placed arrangements of stones, shallow pools and clusters of shrubs reminiscent of a Japanese landscape, while the principal façades, arranged as pavilions, rest on huge lawns that provide carefully orchestrated vistas to artworks and street furniture.

Hampshire Corporate Park
continued over page

Hampshire Corporate Park
continued

A view from the head of a fire escape staircase sees the architecture waiting for a landscape to mature, whereas the entrance pavilion to building number four at Chandler's Ford, is served by a shallow pool and artwork which can more easily be contemporary with the architecture it serves.

Chester Business Park

LOCATION: Chester, Cheshire, England

NAME OF PROJECT: 'Pavilions'

FUNCTION OF BUILDING: High-technology units

DATE OF COMPLETION: 1988

ARCHITECT: Ormrod and Partners, Liverpool, England

'Pavilions' is part of English Estates' Chester Business
Park development.

Chester Business Park
continued over page

Chester Business Park
continued

Callendar Business Park

LOCATION: Falkirk, Scotland

NAME OF PROJECT: Callendar Business Park

SIZE: 42,000m²

FUNCTION OF BUILDING: Offices

DATE OF COMPLETION: 1992

ARCHITECT: Jestico + Whiles, London, England

Having declared some support for the quality that can be maintained in prefabricated and proprietary building systems, this project set in an 11-acre park is testimony to the quality of on-site finishes that can be achieved when a high level of rigour is invested in production information and on-site supervision. Although the architecture is mannerist in its rearrangement of basement, piano nobile and attic, with huge windows sitting without a base and breaking through the lower course, the simplicity and elegance of the composition allows the architecture to triumph over the pedagogy of the tripartite arrangement of traditional Scottish architecture.

Callender Business Park
continued over page

Callendar Business Park continued

Peel Park

LOCATION: East Kilbride, Lanarkshire, Scotland

NAME OF PROJECT: Donprint Building

FUNCTION OF BUILDING: Office building

DATE OF COMPLETION: 1990

ARCHITECT: Dai Rees Associates, Glasgow, Scotland

The Donprint building, unrepresentative of Peel Park
architecture as a whole refers to the 'stately home in a
park' idea.

Dundee Technology Park

LOCATION: Dundee, Scotland

NAME OF PROJECT: The Grianan Building

SIZE: 1,494m^2

FUNCTION OF BUILDING: Speculative technology building

DATE OF COMPLETION: 1987

ARCHITECT: Nicoll Russell, Dundee, Scotland

The Dundee Technology Park in Scotland is small in comparison with the second, third and fourth generation parks now being developed in Europe and America. However, every part of the Grianan building is beautifully considered with the archaeology of the site, not only establishing a dynamic counterpoint between the steel-framed building and its cross wall, but also establishing a subtle and sophisticated collage between the natural and the man-made. Rather than establish a new and essentially artificial landscape, the Grianan building, together with its neighbours, have been carefully inserted into an indigenous environment .

Cody Business Centre

LOCATION: London, England

NAME OF PROJECT: 7 Cody Road

SIZE: 13,000m²

FUNCTION OF BUILDING: Production and distribution

DATE OF COMPLETION: 1989

ARCHITECT: Thorpe Architecture, Arundel, West Sussex, England

Within the realm of low and medium budget buildings, the evolution of the factory aesthetic has promoted an architectural language of curtain walling and profiled metal decking. Combined with silver guard bumpers, pop-out round cornered windows and powerful graphics, the architecture of the Cody Business Centre in London refers closely to the language of the heavy automobile industry.

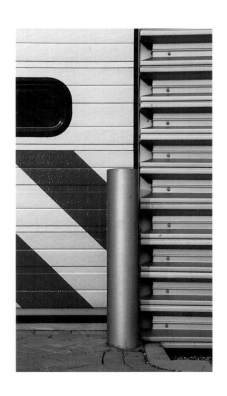

County Oak

LOCATION: Crawley, West Sussex, England

NAME OF PROJECT: Lindbergh House (County Oak 2)

SIZE: 27,000m² (approximately)

FUNCTION OF BUILDING: Flexible office space

DATE OF COMPLETION: 1990

ARCHITECT: Thorpe Architecture, Arundel, West Sussex, England

The large range of proprietary building systems for applications within the field of office research and light industrial buildings has found architects establishing a sub-language system that almost wholly comprises the application, manipulation and inventive rearrangement of customized, mass-produced architectural elements.

Auckland Park

LOCATION: Milton Keynes, Buckinghamshire, England
NAME OF PROJECT: Auckland Park
SIZE: 50,000m^2
FUNCTION OF BUILDING: Speculative office campus
DATE OF COMPLETION: 1990 (Phase I)
ARCHITECT: Sansome Hall, Milton Keynes,
Buckinghamshire, England

This is a three-phase campus development, with parking
for 500 cars and a formalised landscape within the
confines of the site. Informal woodland surrounds the
development.

The architecture of first generation business parks
deliberates between the aesthetic languages of industrial
buildings and commercial buildings. At the Auckland
Business Park, modest panelled structures are dressed
with an ectoskeletal system of roof supports, *brises-soleil*
and exterior fabric maintenance decks.

Blackbrook Business Park

LOCATION: Taunton, Somerset, England

SIZE: 500,000ft^2; 166,000m^2 (Master Plan)

FUNCTION OF BUILDING: Speculative office buildings

DATE OF COMPLETION: Proposal status

ARCHITECT: ORMS Designers and Architects, London, England

This is a masterplan for a four-phase speculative development of 500,000ft^2 of B1 office space at junction 25 of the M5. The grouping of the buildings into a series of 'business villages' allows a significant presence for landscaping to be achieved.

Centre Park

LOCATION: Warrington, Cheshire, England

SIZE: 12 acres; Phase 1 buildings; 30,000m² in eight buildings

FUNCTION OF BUILDING: Speculative office and light industrial building

DATE OF COMPLETION: August 1990

ARCHITECT: ORMS Designers and Architects, London, England

The site comprises 73 acres of former industrial land and playing fields and it has been opened up by the creation of a 12 acre linear park down its centre. Planning consent exists for mixed use on a variety of sites surrounding the park giving flexibility to respond to market need.

Letchworth Business Park

LOCATION: Letchworth, Hertfordshire, England

SIZE: 54 acres

NAME OF PROJECT: Business Centre West

FUNCTION OF BUILDING: Offices for high-tech companies

DATE OF COMPLETION: 1986

ARCHITECT: DY Davies Associates, Richmond, Surrey, England

As business parks become a recognized archetype, language systems develop to identify the low cost architecture of speculative office and research buildings.

Often, a light steel frame is clad in a proprietary system of modular infill and glazing panels, that rely on a sophisticated system of detailing to promote the product beyond the mere utility of construction.

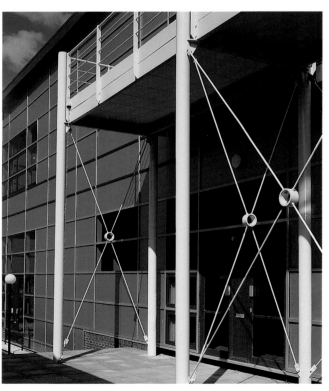

Bricklayers Arms

LOCATION: London, England

NAME OF PROJECT: Bricklayers Arms

SIZE: 18,870m²

FUNCTION OF BUILDING: Warehouse/industrial units

DATE OF COMPLETION: 1992

ARCHITECT: David Richmond & Partners, London, England

The development combines seven industrial warehouse units with wide-loading parking areas (full circles for articulated lorries) and open-plan office space.

Although not a park in the traditional and revised sense of the word, the new factory warehouses built by David Richmond and Partners in central London use frames in space, screen walls and architectonic markers to imply a type of enclosure and place making, the quality of which is uncommon in many conventional out-of-city first generation business parks. The combination of steel and masonry, together with the quality of construction, detailing and architectural composition raises what might have been a development only distinguished by its ordinariness to an architectural statement of considerable quality.

Bricklayers Arms continued over page

Bricklayers Arms continued

Thames Valley Park

LOCATION: Reading, Berkshire, England

NAME OF PROJECT: British Gas Building

SIZE: 20,550m^2

FUNCTION OF BUILDING: Headquarters and offices

DATE OF COMPLETION: 1990

ARCHITECT: Broadway Malyan, Addlestone, Surrey, England

British Gas exploration and products divisions now owner-occupy the first phase of Thames Valley Park. The brief called for a high quality office development in an exceptionally well landscaped setting. The three buildings are of a 'family' in terms of materials and detailing, but differences in form and their enclosure of space give them individual identities. Modern and architecturally crisp, but able to fit into a green landscape, the polished blockwork is complemented and contrasted with curtain walling, metal cladding and slate roofs.

The business park at Thames Valley comprises a small family of three buildings which altogether homogenized by a common palette of materials comprising polished blockwork, curtain walling, metal cladding and slate roofs, are distinguished by differences in form and enclosure. The semi-mature and existings landscape allows the relatively new buildings to sit in a conventional and ruralized park environment.

The Second Generation: Business and Community

In conventional business districts that have been established by history rather than design, the making of a community is embedded in the natural morphology of city life. In downtown areas, cafés, sports clubs, banks and shops interface with commerce to support the needs of a nine-to-five community. In their absence, business precincts become ghettos by day and ghosts by night, to suffer the same alienation that beset the mass housing developments of the 1960s and 1970s, which were eventually destroyed by a lack of community support facilities.

Having learnt from these lessons, architects and developers have created new building briefs that avoid the shortfalls of first generation parks and combine the qualities of successful downtown community life to make commercial developments which, although small, attempt to create a sense of place and society. Such is a second generation park – not large enough in scale and density to achieve the critical mass that can afford large amenity complexes and high ratios of non-developable open space, but of a type and quality that simultaneously integrates the business park into the urban or suburban matrix as a positive contribution to an existing community and maintains a self-contained identity with which the corporate population can identify.

The most successful second generation parks do not isolate themselves on the edge of a freeway outside of great cities. More often, they fill voids left in urban perimeters to re-engage and revitalize suburban identities, or to re-characterize the visual blight left by earlier light industries made redundant by new technologies. These gateway developments often quote urban

space typologies as the key to their design intentions. The Irvine Spectrum Freeway buildings in California comprise speculative research buildings ranged around a network of interconnecting open spaces that succeed in providing community areas, and are described as 'outdoor rooms'.

In the west London suburb of Chiswick, the visionary and innovative British developer, Stuart Lipton, has brought together leading architects, including Sir Norman Foster and Sir Richard Rogers, to make a second generation park over 33 acres that will become a paradigm for an emerging architectural building type – the *multi-building building* – that is at the centre of all the principal qualities and criteria comprising the best in business parks. With the anchor of a centralized and formal open space that is referential to the urban scale of Berkeley Square, the American landscape architect Laurie Olin has responded to the indigenous fabric of Chiswick by weaving avenues, lakes and open community areas around a group of office and amenity buildings that are individual to the aesthetic position of each architect, and yet homogenized by a holistic planning and architectural philosophy that subscribes to the developed axiom that good architecture is good business.

Rather than attempting to establish a new community on the boundary of – or outside – the city limits, Chiswick Place and other second generation parks seek to bring commerce back from the country. They are intended to become formal and recognizable city planning components, as much a natural part of suburban life as the traditional structures of housing, shopping, leisure, schools and theatre.

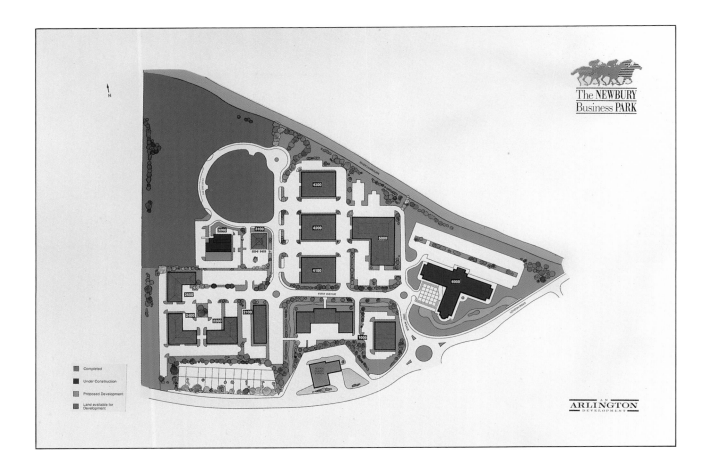

Newbury Business Park

LOCATION: Newbury, Berkshire, England

SIZE: 30 acres

DATE OF COMPLETION: Ongoing

MASTER PLAN: Thorpe Architecture, Arundel, West Sussex, England

In smaller, second generation parks that might attract very divergent commercial tenants there is always the possibility of contrasting architectural expressions being in very close proximity. Hence the glass panel and neoprime architecture of the ATS Building by Thorpe Architecture (right) is in marked contrast to the rather pretentious language of its Cabletron neighbour (far right) by Lyons, Sleaman & Hoare.

ATS Building: Thorpe Architecture

Cabletron Building: Lyons, Sleaman & Hoare

Digital Building: Thorpe Architecture

Newbury Business Park continued

One of the principal advantages in using proprietary lightweight cladding and panel systems is that the quality can be monitored during the factory process. Instead of the quality fluctuations found in on-site wet trade construction, factory-made units depend only on the efficiency of a tried and tested machine and jig operation. At the Newbury Business Park, pre-finished colour coating also ensure consistency of finish, long term maintenance free periods and an architectonic quality to the visual language that is consistent through drawing, production and realization.

Similarly, the ordinariness of a repetitive curtain wall system of the Digital Building (above), framed well by a stream and maturing landscape is in sharp contrast to the brick and stone gridded language of its neighbour, 6000 Rivergate (right).

6000 Rivergate: Skidmore, Owings & Merrill

Arlington Business Park

LOCATION: Theale, Reading, Berkshire, England

SIZE: 48 acres

NAME OF PROJECT: Phase One Building

FUNCTION OF BUILDING: Headquarters Offices

DATE OF COMPLETION: 1990

ARCHITECT: The Fitzroy Robinson Partnership, London, England

A linear group of buildings is ranged about a large lake as a light formation of pavilions, sometimes dropping into the water as if in a Japanese tradition. Although modest in form, a simple frame establishes an homogeneous geomancy against an asymmetrical landscape.

Vision Park

LOCATION: Histon, Cambridgeshire, England
SIZE: 70,000m^2
FUNCTION OF BUILDING: Office buildings
DATE OF COMPLETION: 1991
ARCHITECT: Tartan Tectonics, Cambridge, England

In contrast to the first generation parks, the buildings
and their landscape are considered as a unified
architectural composition. A masonry-clad frame
establishes a principal order about which the primary
staircase and entrance hall are juxtaposed. Bridges,
arbours and artworks frame a balancing pond that
reflects the buildings to create an holistic composition of
richness and ambiguity.

Valley View Commerce Center

LOCATION: Santa Fe Springs, California, USA

NAME OF PROJECT: Valley View Commerce Center

SIZE: 71,000m^2

FUNCTION OF BUILDING: MIxed-use business center

DATE OF COMPLETION: 1990

ARCHITECT: Leason Pomeroy Associates, Irvine, California, USA

Set in a severe industrial environment, this project brings an upscale attitude towards light industrial mixed-use projects to a relatively conservative area.

The design philosophy centres around a street-like setting and maintains a simple programme with a symmetrical plan. Additionally, architectural feature elements are used to add interest, utilizing accent colours, punctured walls, and graduated grid patterned pavements complemented with lush landscaping, to create a pleasant, professional, and efficient environment. Gabled and arched rooflines are also utilized in the design; imagery reminiscent traditional industrial buildings.

Special attention is given to a difficult lease space by creating a plaza atmosphere, adding pyramidal skylights, and enhancing the peripheral landscape.

Irvine Spectrum Freeway

LOCATION: Irvine, California, USA

NAME OF PROJECT: Irvine Spectrum Freeway
Buildings

SIZE: 56,000m²

FUNCTION OF BUILDING: Speculative research and
development building

DATE OF COMPLETION: 1989

ARCHITECT: Leason Pomeroy Associates, Irvine,
California, USA

Located in a 400-acre master planned development of
industrial and R & D space, this speculative research and
development project was intended to continue
California's rich tradition of tilt-up concrete innovation.
Since the earliest works of Irving Gill and R. M. Schnidler
the use of tilt-up, as a cost-efficient method of
construction, has always been pioneered and artfully
considered in California. The design intent was to
continue this tradition of innovation by telling a story of
how tilt-up concrete can be used structurally and
expressed aesthetically.

By varying the construction of the tilt-up panels, from
the street façades to the freeway exposure, a dialogue is
created with the construction technology that begins to
talk about the potential of tilt-up as a design element.

Antrim Technology Park

LOCATION: Antrim, Co Antrim, Northern Ireland

SIZE: 897m²

NAME OF PROJECT: Advanced Software Centre

FUNCTION OF BUILDING: Software manufacture

DATE OF COMPLETION: 1990

ARCHITECT: Kennedy, FitzGerald and Associates, Belfast, Northern Ireland

Antrim Technology Park continued over page

Antrim Technology Park continued

Antrim Technology Park
continued

The Software Centre at the Antrim Technology Park is
referential to a pavilion typology, with a light filigree
order of columns and *brises-soleils* set into a cleft in the
landscape that reduces the building's scale to that of its
single-storey neighbours.

Eden Park

LOCATION: Fenstanton, Cambridgeshire, England
SIZE: 26 acres
FUNCTION OF BUILDING: Office buildings
DATE OF COMPLETION: Proposal status
ARCHITECT: Tartan Tectonics, Cambridge, England

The small development at Eden Park turns its back on the access road to offer up a crescent of seven car parking lots of varying sizes. The buildings enclose two sides of a large lake that in turn gives way to the open countryside. The layering of highway, tree-screen, car park building and water is typical of many small parks that see no advantage in presenting their front doors to the traffic access corridor.

New Square

LOCATION: Bedfont Lakes, Heathrow, London, England

SIZE: 18 acres

FUNCTION OF BUILDING: Office campus of seven office buildings totalling 115,000m^2

DATE OF COMPLETION: 1992

ARCHITECT: Edward Cullinan Architects and Michael Hopkins & Partners, London, England

New Square, in fact, comprises two squares, each built on only three sides. Two separate architects were commissioned to enclose the squares which, by placing the car parking in the centre of the square and landscaping between the buildings and the central section, are direct inversions of traditional model, although the developers claim that the new square is 'rooted in the classic tradition of formally planned buildings'.

New Square continued over page

New Square continued

The Michael Hopkins buildings sit authoritatively on a field within a natural landscape of wetlands and mature trees. The strength of the composition as it addresses the open countryside lies directly in its lack of compromise. The second group of buildings are referential to more traditional building materials and construction methods with contemporary interpretations of traditional architectural formalisms. When the Hopkins' flourish of lightweight tensile technology is laid over Edward Cullinan's conservatism, the surreal juxtaposition further comprises homogeneity of potentially engaging scheme.

Chiswick Master Plan

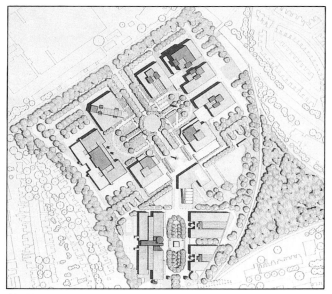

Chiswick Overhead Site Model

94

Chiswick Place

LOCATION: Chiswick, London, England

DATE OF COMPLETION: Proposal status

MASTER PLAN: Terry Farrell Partnership Ltd, London, England

For every major development such as the proposed business park in Chiswick, West London, there is both a planning agenda and a social agenda in planning terms, the site is ideal, not only by virtue of its proximity to the international airport at Heathrow and the M4 motorway, together with doorstep connections to bus, underground and rail systems, but also because of its pivotal position in one of the principal West London suburbs as to form what the developers define as a 'gateway development', whereby the physical form of the development establishes a landmark interface between downtown metropolitan London and suburbia.

In social terms, the park is conceived as part of a regeneration programme for an arera of London that will benefit from the community and employment opportunities that can be resourced by the commercial facilities of a business park. With a skilful Master Plan that embodies a careful balance between public and private realms within a landscape of squares, avenues and plazas, the business and the broader communities really benefit.

Foster Associates Building

Foggo Associates Building

Chiswick Place continued

Preliminary study models for two of the proposed
buildings at Chiswick demonstrate the high level of
architectural patronage existing within the philosophy of
the business park developers – Stanhope Properties
Limited. Both square on plan, the Norman Foster
building reveals an entrance atrium by way of a diagonal
bisection that brings light into centre of the building to
reveal vertical circulation units and the principal
reception. The steel and glass building by Peter Foggo
Associates is provided with solar protection and a
maintenance access desk by an actoskeletal lattice of
white steel work capped by a cantilevered brise-soleil.

Ahrends, Burton and Koralek Building

Chiswick Place continued

Another study model by Ahrends, Burton and Koralek
shows a four-storey steel and curtain walled building
emerging from behind a brick screen wall that identifies
the entrance and has the composition achieve a level of
monolithy. Circular fire escape and stairtowers are
canopied and clad in perforated metal. These and the
light-framed entrance mast help to pin the composition
together, as well as establishing formal tectonic
counterpoints.

The Third Generation:
Developing the Neighbourhood
The three elements distinguishing third generation developments from an emerging family of business parks are scale, location and density. It is inevitable for good ideas to grow, and for the suburban park to develop conceptually to a point that required parcels of land unavailable within the recognized boundaries of a city conurbation. But as the concept grew, the criteria shifted.

In a suburban location, density and car parking ratios are designed according to the availability of public transport systems. Indeed, the strength of the second generation concept lies in the compatibility of location and transport, particularly the fact that employees in the park can travel to and from work by foot, bicycle, bus *and* car. Low cost land available for a park of 100 to 500 acres is found by dormitory areas or near to airports that are themselves dislocated from the city centre. Consequently, the major access transport is the motor car which itself becomes part of the business park marketing package, and a major factor in the density equation.

Scale determines location, location determines transport, and transport influences density. If the third generation business park cannot make a contribution to the city, there is enormous potential for gains to be had in the low-density developments of those ubiquitous parcels of derelict or blighted land that sit beyond the suburb but before the open country. And the gain is considerable, given that some business parks have a building

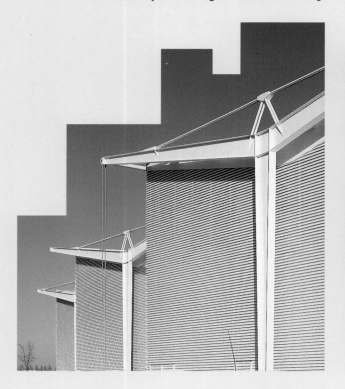

floorplate to open space ratio of 25% to 30%, whereby the *park* is far larger than the *business*. Stockley Park, at Heathrow, England, is an extraordinary example of planning, public and business gain. The site was originally quarried to provide clay for the bricks of London. The refuse created by the houses built with the brick went back to fill the hole made by the quarry. After years of compaction, the huge rubbish tip became an environmental disaster. Bought by the developers Stanhope, the rubbish was cleared, neighbours were protected by a tube of perfume that surrounded the site during clearance work, and a new business neighbourhood was created within a park of trees, lakes, lawns and wildlife. In addition, an 18-hole championship golf course, equestrian centre and sports fields were built and given back to the community via the local city hall.

At a large scale, the third generation park can contribute to the private and public realms, while providing those types of advanced technology businesses that could not function optimally within an inner city environment with an ideal landscape in which to perform.

Capability Green

LOCATION: Luton Hoo, Luton, Bedfordshire, England

SIZE: 283,290m^2

DATE OF COMPLETION: 1988

MASTER PLAN: Bruce Gilbreth Architects Ltd, London, England

The masterplan for Capability Green's business park sets up primary, secondary and tertiary axes that refer to a hierarchical disposition of building types.

Although many parks refer to a romantic paradigm, Capability Green, by way of a quintessential irony, marks out linear routes and circuits through structured and formal devices that are more Italian in origin than English.

Capability Green continued over page

Capability Green continued

NAME OF PROJECT: Anritsu Europe Ltd

SIZE: 2,045m^2

FUNCTION OF BUILDING: HQ and laboratory space

DATE OF COMPLETION: 1988

ARCHITECT: Bruce Gilbreth Architects Ltd, London, England

The short days of a typically British winter make it important for buildings to be as attractive by night as they are by day. Smooth prefabricated cladding systems over a modest and low budget structural frame reflect the external low level ambient light whilst the task and spotlighting both to the open office areas and access stairs create a juxtaposed complexity.

B

proposed
Phase 3A

STOCKLEY PARK ↑
LANDSCAPE MASTER PLAN
0 25 50   100m

Stockley Park

LOCATION: Heathrow, London, England

SIZE: 400 acres

DATE OF COMPLETION: 1986 and ongoing

MASTER PLAN: Arup Associates, London, England

The landscape Master Plan for Stockley Park clearly
demonstrates the generosity of environmental gain
when the building footprint is judged against the scale of
the overall development. A principal frustration for the
vision of business park developers and their architects is
the time difference between the commercial necessity
for a fast-track building programme and the relatively
slower progress of mother nature.

Stockley Park continued over page

Stockley Park continued

Three million cubic metres of rubbish was cleared from the Stockley Park site (below) and new levels restored by the importation of 1.5 cubic metres of building sub-base. It is an extraordinary testimonial to the vision of developers Stanhope that such extreme dereliction could be understood to have the potential of a commercial arcadia.

Long Walk Road Lake

Stockley Park continued over page

Roundwood Avenue Lake

5 Long Walk Road: Foster Associates

6 Furzeground Way: Eric Parry Associates

Stockley Park continued

The landscaping matrix comprised a network of
balancing lakes to secure the physics of an economic
water management system embraced by a linear string
of planting.

A stream runs past the Sir Norman Foster building
(left), connecting to balancing ponds to discharge
eventually as a flat plate of water over which the Eric
Parry building sits (above). The traditions and
morphologies of the water element in architectural
composition have been fully understood and embraced
within the Stockley Park Master Plan. The lakes, streams
and wetlands combined to serve the park with an
environment that can metamorphose from recreation to
meditation within a few hundred metres.

Stockley Park continued over page

Stockley Park continued

NAME OF PROJECT: The Arena

SIZE: 5,912m^2

FUNCTION OF BUILDING: Central amenity building

DATE OF COMPLETION: 1986

ARCHITECT: Arup Associates, London, England

Third generation parks such as Stockley are able to achieve a critical mass whereby the size of the development can afford recreational and other support systems. Visitors to Stockley Park are greeted by the highest of the balancing lakes, the far end of which is marked by a building containing sports club, shops, restaurants, wine bars, banks and other support facilities. Called the Arena, the building has a modest, yet heroic quality to it, with a predominately load-bearing masonry construction giving way to a glass and steel gazebo that functions as a brasserie. When lit, the brasserie is transformed into a beacon, identifying the location of the Arena for the business community and visitors alike.

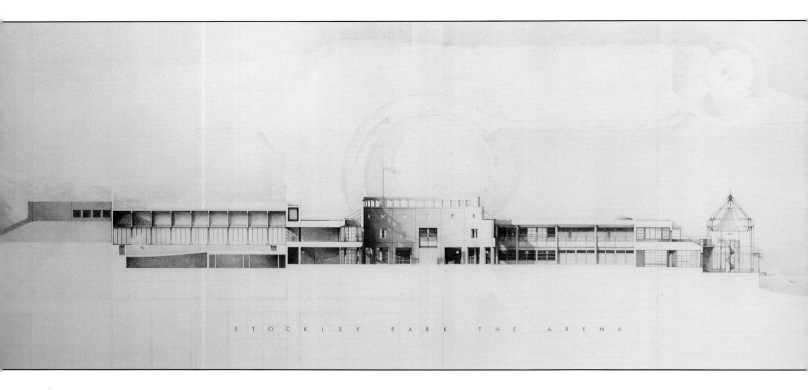

STOCKLEY PARK THE ARENA

Stockley Park continued over page

The Arena

Stockley Park continued

The Arena continued

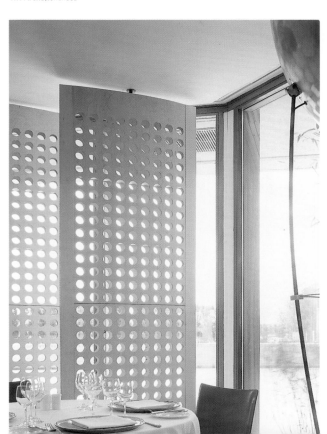

Stockley Park

NAME OF PROJECT: The Arena Restaurant

DATE OF COMPLETION: 1986

ARCHITECT: Beardsmore Associates with Arup Associates, London, England

The beautifully crafted interior of the main restaurant in the Stockley Park amenity building is marked by a series of curved and perforated aerofoil screens that pivot top and bottom either to release views to the balancing lake beyond or to perform as *brises-soleil*. The undulated suspended ceiling sets up a powerful counterpoint to the reflective horizontal floor platform that reflects the pinhead spotlighting. Large polished steel dishes supported on braced armatures wash light over the fair-face blockwork internal walls that serve to re-quote the external language of the Arena complex, as well as mediate between the polished masonry floor and a timber ceiling.

Stockley Park continued over page

Stockley Park continued

NAME OF PROJECT: 5 Long Walk Road

SIZE: 40,160m²

FUNCTION OF BUILDING: BP Exploration offices

DATE OF COMPLETION: 1990

ARCHITECT: Foster Associates, London, England

The developers of Stockley Park believe that there is a connection between commercial success and architectural quality. Within a prevailing philosophy that supports the dictum that good architecture equals good business, Stockley Park Consortium Ltd., have commissioned some of the world's leading architects to design individual pieces within the framework of an overall masterplan. The Norman Foster building is a paradigm to the act of faith given by the site owners to architects that are normally associated with high-profile projects. The structural matrix as expressed at the front and rear of each pavilion comprises a central post supporting a pair of braced armatures that are tied down at their boundaries with tension cables. The crafting of this principal element extends beyond the envelope to function as a *brise-soleil* over a curtain wall of Austrian fritted glass.

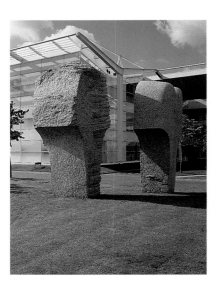

The light transparency of the British Petroleum building is in sharp contrast to an artwork by the sculptor Stephen Cox. His work 'Osirifisis' was fashioned by the splitting and working of a huge Egyptian stone by way of establishing oblique symbolic references to matters including the witnessing of creation. Chief Executive Stuart Lipton has the same commitment to art as he does to architecture. When excellence of each kind is brought together in the context of a business park, it secures a theory that property development can be an intellectual, culture and commercial activity.

Stockley Park continued over page

Stockley Park continued

NAME OF PROJECT: 3 Furzeground Way

SIZE: 7,645m^2

FUNCTION OF BUILDING: Speculative 'flex' space

DATE OF COMPLETION: 1990

ARCHITECT: Ian Ritchie Architects, London, England

The multi-let building by Ian Ritchie examines the potential of a glass curtain wall system designed as a continuous transparent skin. The relentless repetition of flush-fixed, near beam jointed glass panels is relieved on three sides of the building by a roof line order of aero-foiled perforated metal sunscreens. The elegant simplicity of the building is at times in contrast to an abstract complexity of shadows and reflections.

Stockley Park continued over page

Stockley Park continued

NAME OF PROJECT: 4 Roundwood Avenue

SIZE: 44,100m^2

FUNCTION OF BUILDING: Electronic Data Systems
building

DATE OF COMPLETION: 1990

ARCHITECT: Arup Associates, London, England

A pair of vertical access towers anchor a free-standing
curved screen to the projecting entrance pavilion of the
Electronic Data Systems building. The three-storey
building behind operates as a passive foil against which
the reflected geometries declare their functional and
aesthetic clarity.

Stockley Park continued over page

Stockley Park continued

NAME OF PROJECTS: 3 and 4 Long Walk Road

SIZE: BP Exploration: 26,000m²; Marks & Spencer: 38,000m²

FUNCTION OF BUILDING: Office and administration for BP Exploration and Marks & Spencer

DATE OF COMPLETION: 1990

ARCHITECT: Arup Associates, London, England

The BP exploration building and the Marks & Spencer's building create a highly textured back-drop to one of many pedestrian routes that provide for the interaction of business and community within a Master Plan of clarity and complexity.

Stockley Park continued

NAME OF PROJECT: 6 Roundwood Avenue

SIZE: 16,800m^2

FUNCTION OF BUILDING: Office and administration for Apple Computers

DATE OF COMPLETION: 1990

ARCHITECT: Troughton MacAslan, London, England

The high level of glazing required to provide a reasonable level of ambient natural lighting to a deep-plan office layout necessitates consideration of the sunscreen issue. At Stockley Park, solutions are as diverse as Austrian fridged glass in the Foster building to projecting perforated metal foils by Ian Ritchie. In their building for Apple Computers, architects Troughton MacAslan solved the problem by stretching a fabric membrane between a series of cantilevered brackets.

Stockley Park continued over page

Stockley Park Phase 2

NAME OF PROJECT: 6 Furzeground Way

SIZE: 12,000m²

FUNCTION OF BUILDING: Speculative 'flex' space

DATE OF COMPLETION: 1991

ARCHITECT: Eric Parry & Associates, London, England

Within the financial conformities of a speculative office building, Eric Parry & Associates have crafted a virtuoso work. The first-floor shell and core is enclosed with bands of glass and glass blocks, functioning by translucency and transparency as sunscreen and window. One wing of the building is rotated away from its identical counterpart, the separation creating room for reception, utilities and a tapering glazed-roofed atrium. This comparatively eccentric figure is characterized by studious detailing and a rich palette of materials including marble wall panels, Cumberland slate floors and a huge mural by Eric Parry himself. The modest formality of the entrance elevation is animated by a pair of weirs that feed one of the southern lakes.

Stockley Park continued over page

Stockley Park Phase 2

NAME OF PROJECT: Project W2
SIZE: 38,000m^2
FUNCTION OF BUILDING: Speculative office space
DATE OF COMPLETION: Ongoing
ARCHITECT: Peter Foggo Associates, London, England

Peter Foggo Associates' study model for one of
the proposed buildings in Phase 2 of the Stockley Park
development is a sophisticated demonstration of
architectural holism. Entrance areas, vertical circulation
systems and utility stacks together with the offices they
serve are all homogenized under a single arched canopy.
As the roof extends beyond the building envelope, a type
of architectonic origami provides for a single idea to
achieve views from other floors, sunscreens and the
visual declaration of the building's structural geomancy.
The visual weight of the building is further diluted about
each of the two short elevations with a concavity of
perforated purlins cantilevering beyond the façade to
support the projecting line of *brise-soleil*.

Vintage Park

LOCATION: Foster City, California, USA

NAME OF PROJECT: Vintage Park

SIZE: 13,000m^2

FUNCTION OF BUILDING: Mixed-use development

DATE OF COMPLETION: 1989

ARCHITECT: Leason Pomeroy Associates, Irvine, California, USA

Vintage Park Lots 1 & 2 are located east of Vintage Park Boulevard within the Vintage Park Master Plan, a mixed-use development in Foster City, California. These two parcels include single-storey light industrial buildings as well as a two-storey office building.

The buildings are constructed of tilt-up concrete panels, featuring an articulated modular grid exterior surface. Exterior facia awnings are utilized in addition to entry plaza features, abundant landscaping, open space, series of fresh-water lagoons, waterways and brick-paved pedestrian pathways which contribute to a park-like 'live-work-and-play' environment.

The project will eventually connect with Foster City's future shoreline bikeway as well as the future residential areas planned into the project.

The 'Master Plan' for the long-range development of Vintage Park, Foster City, is a paramount importance. The requirement was to create a unique and exciting mixed-use development that would respect the conditions that exist yet have the qualities of urban life, be conducive to public use, ensure safety, welfare and recreation, and relate to the contemporary life styles of Foster City's personal community.

In keeping with Foster City's approach and heritage, the character will be embodied in a 'park-like' setting, reflecting the water-orientated theme of Foster City. Major land uses of offices, commercial/retail, research and development buildings and other support facilities are planned and integrated within the overall framework. This basic framework consists of a series of interlocking systems that contain generous landscaping, creations of fresh-water features, and circulation systems which include bicycle paths, pedestrian and transit connections; visual order, interest and spatial sequence; and public safety.

Tri-City Landing

LOCATION: San Bernardino, California, USA

SIZE: 40,000m²

DATE OF COMPLETION: Ongoing

ARCHITECT: Leason Pomeroy Associates, Irvine, California, USA

This site, situated prominently on the north bank of a major water feature and 'piazza', is the focus of a 160-acre business park. The location of this theme building and the future phases of the Master Plan are organized around the piazza and water feature in a way that creates a unique new quality and identity for the entire development. This project's design takes advantage of these site influences and orientation, producing a building which responds to its context, reinforcing the ideas of a special place in this development.

Landmark Square

LOCATION: Tempe, Arizona, USA

NAME OF PROJECT: Landmark Square

SIZE: 190,000m²

FUNCTION OF BUILDING: Mixed-use commercial district

DATE OF COMPLETION: Ongoing

ARCHITECT: Leason Pomeroy Associates, Irvine, California, USA

The brief was to create an identifiable 'downtown business and retail district' that would help in the efforts to revitalize the city of Tempe.

The response was to integrate uses and activities that were commonly associated with a downtown central business district-office, retail, restaurant, and theatre space. The components of this proposal included a retail block with enclosed galleria, central atrium with an amphitheatre, office buildings, and a multi-level parking structure.

In developing an architectural language, the architects have borrowed from some of the older historic buildings in Tempe – namely the two and three-storey brick commercial buildings of the late nineteenth and early twentieth century. These buildings have a distinct character, scale and charm, important to the image and personality of downtown Tempe.

Aztec West

LOCATION: Almondsbury, Bristol, Avon, England

SIZE: 157 acres

DATE OF COMPLETION: Ongoing

MASTER PLAN: Thorpe Architecture, Arundel, West Sussex, England

The Master Plan for a large commercial development on the edge of the city of Bristol in southwest England is typical of a well-considered, third generation business park. Direct access from a principal motorway leads to an inner ring road that embraces a number of large-scale developments focussed upon the central amenity building. Five exits from the ring road lead to a group of neighbourhoods, each of which comprise individual building communities of varying scales, densities and compositions.

Whereas the principal central area is anchored by the Aztec West complex, which provides social, recreational and administrative facilities for the whole park, the office village neighbourhood is grouped around a village green. Here, a hotel and pub sets up a different kind of focus. Together, all five neighbourhoods comprise a homogeneous development where individuality within the corporate plan is established by individual architectural pieces. The aerial photograph demonstrates the siting criteria for a 'third generation park', bounded on one side by a motorway and being next to both a dormitory housing development and an existing industrial estate.

Aztec West continued over page

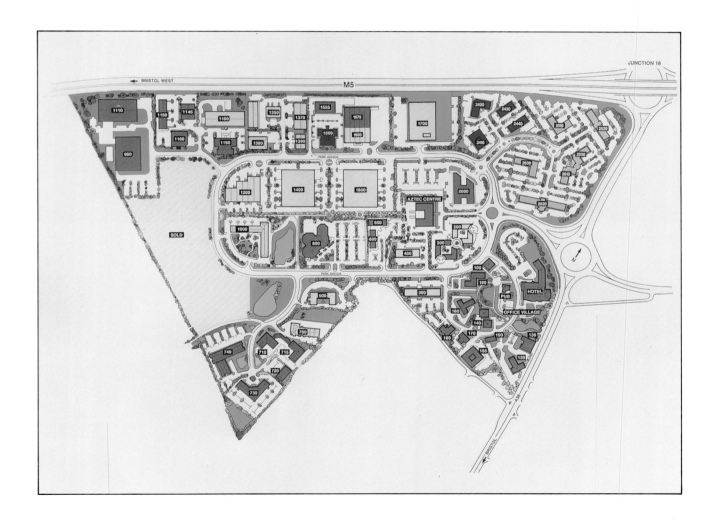

Aztec Centre: Thorpe Architecture

Aztec West 1200: John Outram Partnership

Aztec West continued

Thorpe Architecture's Aztec Centre provides centralized
amenities for the business community and is positioned
as a stop vista to a formal access from the site entry.
Other buildings on the site, such as a group by John
Outram (left), comply with the demands of the Master
Plan for a comprehensive development while setting up
an architectural language of individuality.

Aztec West continued over page

Aztec West continued

Much of the skill in designing buildings for business parks is in understanding how the building can arbitrate between the park and the parking. The modest, two-storey structure of the Inmos Building (right) settles well into a quickly maturing landscape, while the structural gymnastics of an ectoskeletal structure (below) for Wiggins Teape forms an appropriately demonstrative canvas for the utilitarian road and service bays.

Wiggins Teape Building: Aukett Associates

Inmos Building: EPR Architects

Aztec West continued over page

Aztec West continued

NAME OF PROJECT: Aztec Centre

SIZE: 8,000m^2

DATE OF COMPLETION: 1989

ARCHITECT: Thorpe Architect, Arundel, West Sussex, England

Aztec West continued over page

Aztec West continued

NAME OF PROJECT: Midland Bank

SIZE: 2,200m^2

FUNCTION OF BUILDING: Computer Data Centre

DATE OF COMPLETION: 1990

ARCHITECT: Thorpe Architecture, Arundel, West Sussex, England

Aztec West continued over page

Midland Bank: Thorpe Architecture

Park Gate: Skidmore Owings and Merrill

Aztec West continued

In contrast to the primary geometrical configuration of Thorpe Architecture's Midland Bank building (left), a restrained compositional exercise in the triangle and square, there are other buildings such as Park Gate (above) that require skill in solving the problems of an eccentric site, which are often the product of a rational masterplanning grid laid over the exigencies of an existing typology.

Aztec West continued over page

Aztec West continued

Reflected in the mirrored wall to the Digital building,
Brian Taggart Associates access stair and utilities tower
brings together vertical silver composite panels, glass
blocks and an ectoskeletal steel frame housing exposed
services in a complex but beautifully crafted counterpoint
to the simple shed behind.

The Park Gate building (left) embraces a city courtyard
that sets up one type of intimacy in contrast to another
established by waterfalls, rocks and shingle beaches.

Digital Building Brian Taggart Associates .

Park Gate Skidmore, Owings and Merrill

Falling water and pebbles

Aztec West continued over page

Aztec West continued

Aztec West continued over page

NAME OF PROJECT: 200 Aztec West

SIZE: 5,130m^2

FUNCTION OF BUILDING: Commercial offices

DATE OF COMPLETION: 1989

ARCHITECT: CZWG Architects, London, England

At Aztec West, like many other parks, there is a new opportunity provided for architects to site a major building in a landscape so that the relatively large areas of non-developable land can create long views to a single piece of architecture. This results in an effect to those easily recalled images of a rural Britain scattered with virtuoso pieces of ancestral architecture. In detail, CZWG's architecture is unique in its consideration of, amongst other things, the motor car. The spirit of the business park is the drive-in office. CZWG have understood this literally by taking two great scoops of a hitherto L-shaped building on plan to have the car literally and theoretically part of the architecture. Against the machine, and bearing in mind its siting at the entrance to the whole development, the building declares a refreshing monolithy in contrast to the paper-thin architecture of curtain walls. Given that the fire escape could not be predetermined, the internal courtyard is cloistered by wsay of a first floor covered walkway that can join all parts of the building to the appropriate collection staircases.

The product of this solution is a promenade sun screen and a greater complexity of tectonic modelling. The buildings are fine examples of how a speculative architecture located within a tight planning matrix and determined by cost control can still be the product of theory, intellectuality and wit.

200 Aztec West continued

Aztec West *continued over page*

Aztec West continued

Reflected in the mirrored wall to the Digital building, Brian Taggart Associates' access stair and utilities tower brings together vertical silver composite panels, glass blocks and an ectoskeletal steel frame housing exposed services in a complex but beautifully crafted counterpoint to the simple shed behind.

The Park Gate building (left) embraces a city courtyard that sets up one type of intimacy in contrast to another established by waterfalls, rocks and shingle beaches.

Sintra Business Park

LOCATION: Sintra, Lisbon, Portugal

SIZE: 24 acres

FUNCTION OF BUILDING: Speculative business park

DATE OF COMPLETION: Proposal status

ARCHITECT: Broadway Malyan, Milton Keynes, Buckinghamshire, England

Portugal's first business park, which is to be developed west of Lisbon, will provide a highly-serviced and landscaped business park of ten units (70,000m) in a rapidly developing area. Upper floors will contain office accommodation/distribution areas. Each building is designed to combine modern technology and traditional Portuguese construction and materials.

154

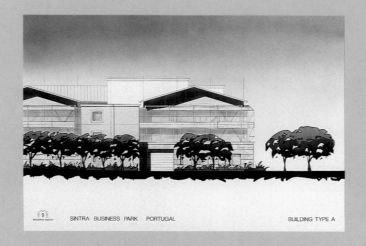

SINTRA BUSINESS PARK PORTUGAL   BUILDING TYPE A

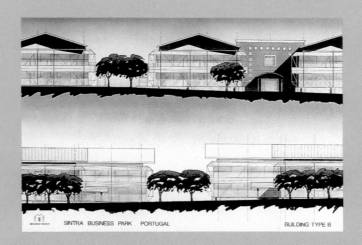

SINTRA BUSINESS PARK PORTUGAL   BUILDING TYPE B

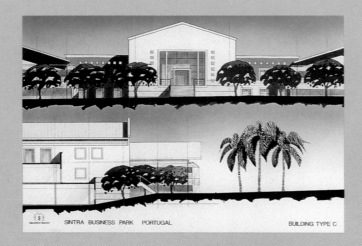

SINTRA BUSINESS PARK PORTUGAL   BUILDING TYPE C

Parque Technologico Del Valles

LOCATION: Ceroanyola, Barcelona, Spain

SIZE: 600m²

NAME OF PROJECT: Hotel-Vivero de Empresas

FUNCTION OF BUILDING: Technology Enterprise Centre

DATE OF COMPLETION: 1989

ARCHITECT: Cristian Cirici & Associats, Barcelona, Spain

A two-storey building is built on a semi-basement with a garage and other installations. It has two bays arranged along a long central corridor with offices to both sides. The construction follows the building perimeter of the site, forming a wide patio in the centre. In the patio, there is a light structure for temporary exhibitions and conferences. This divides the central grand patio into two different areas for easier access.

The enterprise centre provides space and a wide range of support services to facilitate the functioning of newly created advanced technology enterprises.

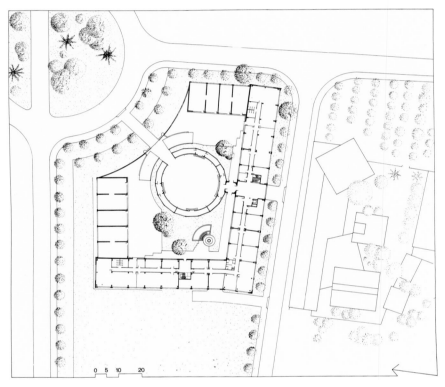

Birmingham Business Park

LOCATION: Solihull, Birmingham, England

DATE OF COMPLETION: Ongoing

SIZE: 148 acres

MASTER PLAN: Auckett Associates, London, England

The position of the Birmingham Business Park again satisfies the principal criteria of siting, being next to the M42 motorway on the outside of a major cosmopolitan city, and yet rural enough to sustain the definition of Park. The Master Plan demonstrates the importance of the water element and its revival as a principal constituent of garden design.

Birmingham Business Park continued over page

Birmingham Business Park
continued

NAME OF PROJECT: Parkside

SIZE: 30,000m^2

FUNCTION OF BUILDING: Speculative 'flex' space

DATE OF COMPLETION: 1990

ARCHITECT: Thorpe Architecture, Arundel, West Sussex,
England

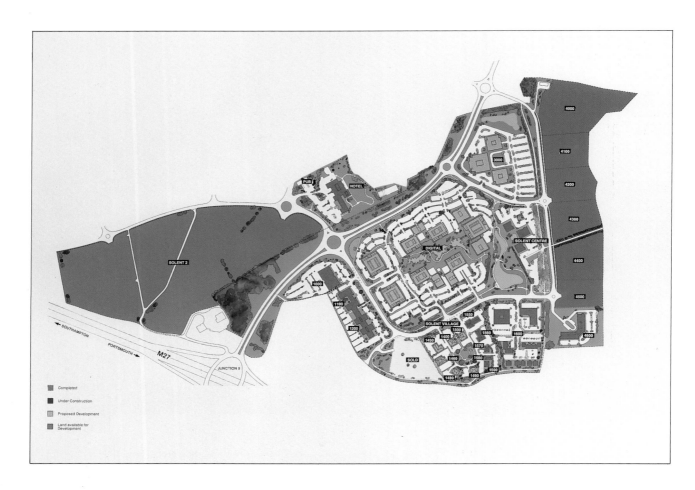

Solent Business Park

LOCATION: Fareham, Hampshire, England

SIZE: 150 acres

DATE OF COMPLETION: Ongoing

MASTER PLAN: Auckett Associates, London, England

The Master Plan for the Solent Business Park is finely crafted to provide a series of small neighbourhoods, each of varying scales and densities, that combine with balancing lakes and open spaces to provide key buildings as stop vistas to long and short views alike. The commitment of developers, Arlington Securities, to both the Grand Plan and minutiae of landscaping detail provides for a working environment that is nourished by both traditional and contemporary examples of English landscape design. In the same way as the business park offers an opportunity for architects to build in the landscape, so they provide an even greater opportunity for the landscape architects to continue the traditions established by Repton and Capability Brown, requiring the type of heroic commitment that was only previously known to the great gardens of stately homes, particularly in the eighteenth and nineteenth centuries.

Solent Business Centre continued over page

Solent Business Park continued

NAME OF PROJECT: Solent Centre

SIZE: 8,595m^2

FUNCTION OF BUILDING: Amenity building

DATE OF COMPLETION: 1990

ARCHITECT: Thorpe Architecture, Arundel, West Sussex, England

The lawns, waterways, paths and parkland frames are all testimony to the business park as the only architectural type that can provide the planner, architect and landscape architect with the same creative opportunities as those provided by the owners of the great eighteenth- and nineteenth-century estates. Thorpe Architecture's modest pavilion for the central amenity building at the heart of the park is framed by mature trees and banks and is reflected in a balancing pond that terminates in a collection of stones. Numerous references to the Japanese tradition of landscape architecture that also became common in many late nineteenth-century gardens paradoxically reinforces the Englishness of these landscape statements.

The Fourth Generation: New Villages

Commercial buildings — especially those dedicated to research, technology and production — are large population projects. With unemployment running high throughout the developed world, the opportunity to welcome a large and comprehensive development of multi-national corporations will often sustain a political enthusiasm within the city halls to relax planning structures and zoning regulations. Consequently, business park developers have used the prospect of enhanced employment potentials to persuade legislators that a multi-use programme, which could include housing, shopping, education and leisure for example, would be an appropriate planning gain. The result is an emerging fourth generation of 'business parks' that are holistic developments providing a self-contained and self-sufficient district of intercommunicating neighbourhoods, the whole of which will become similar to a high-technology village or small town. Whereas the third generation parks evolved from carefully zoned industrial or business estates attached to the perimeter of new towns, the fourth generation has closed the circle to become a new town in itself.

The 183-acre Marina Village development, on the Oakland Estuary at Alameda, California, is a finely crafted Master Plan that includes offices, research and development buildings and retail to anchor the commercial feasibility of the project. Ranged around a drive-in movie theatre, the landscaped business neighbourhood encloses the boundary of housing located on five peninsulas and surrounded by a reclaimed lagoon. To the south, Marina Park separates a group of hotels and restaurants from the 'village' plaza, in the form of a causeway that protects the lagoon from the yachting marina and estuary beyond. In all, it will be possible to work, rest and play within a single complex that declares an

architectural homogeneity which celebrates the historical context of the past, and an arcadian vision of the future, with the relationship of the new village and the wider community secured by a generosity of public leisure and recreational facilities. It is this relationship – between the self-contained security of a fourth generation park and its neighbours – that is the most fragile.

In second generation suburban or gateway developments, the relationship between the park and the surrounding community is *a priori*. In fourth generation schemes, a relationship need not exist for the *village* to claim success, but in Kent, England, the American developers Rouse & Associates, in partnership with the County Council, have considered the need for this relationship carefully, not only in terms of the Kings Hill Park and its contextual milieu, but also the commercial success of the development as a whole. Whereas Marina Village seals a friendship with its neighbours through the olive branch of recreation, Kings Hill plans to secure its social democratization through education. A quadripartite body will be created between the County Council, two British colleges and an American University. There will be an intended reciprocity between the needs of business and the educational resource base with students, academies, employees and residents and public all enjoying a man-made rural idyll in the heart of the British countryside.

As with all fourth generation parks, there is a need for a highly sophisticated level of social engineering. At best, these great parks – if restricted in number – can become landmarks of county and statewide importance and value. At worst, and by an innate sense of territorial prerogative, the fourth generation village will become the new paradise, walled and defended like the parks of Persian kings and nobles.

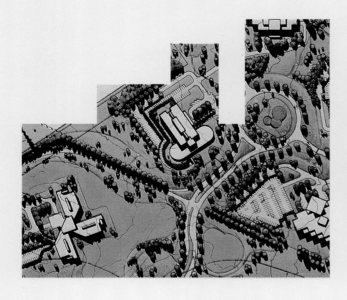

Greenway Business Park

LOCATION: Richardson, Texas, USA

NAME OF PROJECT: Northern Telecom/Bell Northern
Research Campus

SIZE: 200,000m^2

FUNCTION OF BUILDING: Corporate HQ and research
and development facilities

DATE OF COMPLETION: 1992

ARCHITECT: Hardy McCullah/MLM Architects Inc.,
Dallas, Texas, USA

The project combines a 16-storey administration block
and a 10,000m^2 research and development laboratory.
Shared amenities include a cafeteria, credit union,
convenience store and health centre.

The early drawings showing a huge, three-storey linear
arrangement of offices and research facilities ranged as
two armatures about an eighty-foot atrium and barrel-
vaulted ceiling, together with the sixteen-storey tower,
come to realisation via the model making process with
extraordinary accuracy.

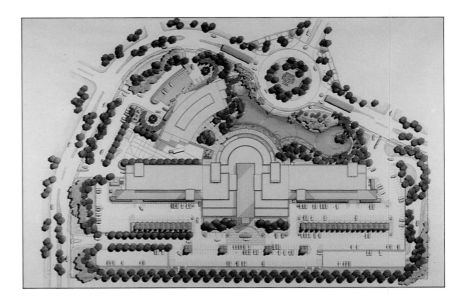

Greenway Business Park continued over page

Greenway Business Park continued

Northern Telecom's Research and Development arm, BNR Incorporated, forms the heart of a huge Texan business park. Unlike European business parks, the scale of development allows for certain areas to be high-rise, including the sixteen storey Northern Telecom tower. Over 4,000 employees call for the inclusion of cafeterias, plazas, shopping and other central facilities, together with the visual and recreational facilities of lakes, gardens and parks. The heroic scale of BNR's complex quietly disguises a highly serviced building of extreme complexity.

Marina Village

LOCATION: Alameda, California, USA

SIZE: 183 acres (land area)

FUNCTION OF BUILDING: Mixed-use project

DATE OF COMPLETION: Ongoing

ARCHITECT: Leason Pomeroy Associates, Irvine, California, USA

This project is designed to suggest a romantic, picturesque 'urban waterfront village', containing retail, commercial and offices uses. All buildings are developed as an integral product, reinforcing the marina village theme.

The overall project will reflect an active, playful, enjoyable environment. Plazas, water features, recreational areas and walkways will be presented in such a way that as one passes from space to space, a new spatial experience is felt by the individual. Areas throughout will contrast from intimate and controlled spaces to open active spaces.

Integral to the project is the linear pedestrian spine which features an historic walk marked by sculptures and plaques; pedestrian streetscapes which will include street vendors, water features, colourful flags and awnings, and picturesque views of downtown Oakland, San Francisco and the Bay Bridge.

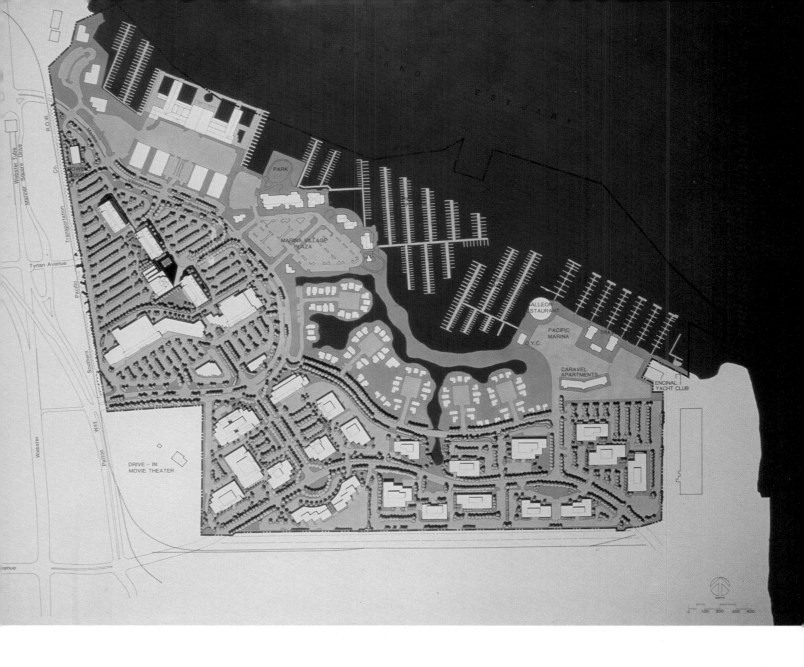

DRIVE – IN
MOVIE THEATER

PARK

MARINA VILLAGE
PLAZA

GALLEON
RESTAURANT

PACIFIC
MARINA

O.Y.C.

TRANSIT

CARAVEL
APARTMENTS

ENCINAL
YACHT CLUB

ESTUARY

Webster Tube
Webster Square Drive
Marina Square Drive
R.O.W.
Constitution ROWER
Transportation
Tynan Avenue
Pacific
Southern
Way
Patton
Webster
Avenue
Village

NORTH
0   100 200 300 400

815

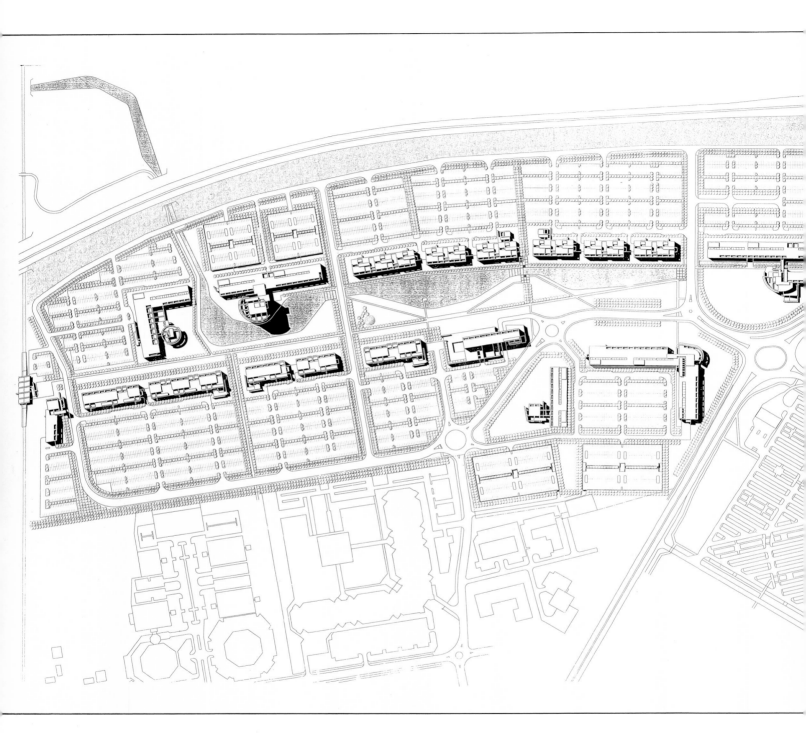

Edinburgh Park

LOCATION: Edinburgh, Scotland

SIZE: 138 acres

DATE OF COMPLETION: Ongoing

MASTER PLAN: Richard Meier, Architect, New York, USA

The Edinburgh business park is ranged around a series of balancing lakes, each of which reflect a formal building type that makes more concessions to the architect's idiomatic devices than it does to either the context, culture, or ethnicity of Scotland.

Kettering Venture Park

LOCATION: Kettering, Northamptonshire, England

SIZE: 92 acres

DATE OF COMPLETION: Ongoing

MASTER PLAN: Mason Richards Partnership, Wolverhampton, West Midlands, England

In addition to the more conventional commercial buildings, the Master Plan at Kettering includes a hotel, restaurant, public house, shopping and housing, all of which provide for the possibilities of a self-contained community. A newly completed building for RCI Europe stands on an elevated platform with the same type of dignity as the traditional English country hosue to which it obviously refers. The opportunity for business parks to create physical images of a stately home for commerce provides a unique opportunity for architects and planners to re-establish the heroic tradition of the large country house.

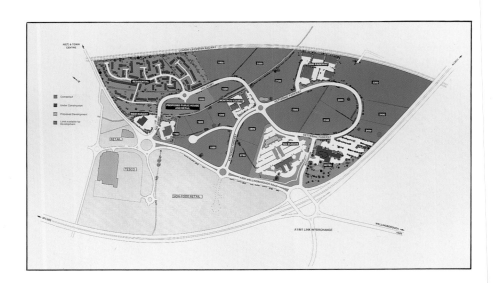

RCI Europe Building: Atkins Lister Drew

Sanden International

LOCATION: Wylie, Texas, USA

NAME OF PROJECT: Sanden International (USA) Inc.

SIZE: 93 acres

FUNCTION OF BUILDING: Corporate campus

DATE OF COMPLETION: 1990 and ongoing

ARCHITECT: Hardy McCullah/MCM Architects Inc., Dallas, Texas, USA

The campus includes manufacturing, research, corporate offices, distribution, housing and recreation. It is planned for future phasing. The architects were awarded the NAIOP Design '90 Honor Award in the Industrial Build-To-Suit category.

Most business parks are characterized by collections or neighbourhoods of buildings, each being occupied by different clients. There is, however, what one might term the single cell or corporate campus where an individual corporation such as the Automotive Air Compressor Company, Sanden, mark out a large territory in which to site their various office research and manufacturing activities. The crescent-shaped administrative building embraces a huge courtyard, itself designed as a metaphor for the activities of the company. Aluminium-faced sandwich panels reinforce the smooth sweep of the research and office facilities, while exposed aggregate concrete declares the robust quality of the manufacturing process behind.

Macarthur Place

LOCATION: Santa Ana, California, USA

NAME OF PROJECT: Macarthur Place

FUNCTION OF BUILDING: Multi-use development

DATE OF COMPLETION: Ongoing

ARCHITECT: Leason Pomeroy Associates, Irvine, California, USA

The architects' design concept was to create a landmark – unlike any other – that symbolize the cultural heritage associated with Orange County.

The Orange County Room has an organizational element with a wave pattern meandering along the plaza highlighted by a glass block 'whitecap' visually representing the crest of a wave, allowing natural lighting to permeate the parking structures below. The room is further enlivened by ocean water features and 'sails' of glass which play against the front doors of each building facing The Room. They create areas within the plaza where street vendors can be organized inserting

activity and excitement to the urban experience.

Water features give another element of interest to The Room, two having ocean analogies while the aqueduct, which springs from the Orange Grove at the termination of The Room, symbolizes the bringing of water to this arid region.

The entry drive presents the two Gatehouse buildings with matching façades, mediators between public and private space. The fenestration of the buildings is a repetition of a vertical jpatterning of solids and voids heightening the sense of passage through the gate.

The Theme Building was distinct in that it is bordered by two major elements, the Water Garden and the Orange County Room. The use of geometry and rooftop gardens gives strength to the composition since the roof is very visible and required special interest.

The Park Portal building establishes the west boundary of the Orange County Room. A path from the urban retail project through this building is highlighted three-dimensionally by a glass canted, six-storey shaft.

Burbank Gateway Center

LOCATION: Burbank, California, USA

NAME OF PROJECT: Burbank Gateway Center

SIZE: 862,000m^2

FUNCTION OF BUILDING: Mixed-use development

DATE OF COMPLETION: Ongoing

ARCHITECT: Leason Pomeroy Associates, Irvine, California, USA

More than a 'regional mall', this mixed-use complex is designed to become the gateway to revitalizing the city. A major hotel facility and office building provides an important balance between retail and commercial development. There will be 7,000 cars parked in fully landscaped structures with clear pedestrian access to all environments. The automobile is treated as an honoured guest in the plan. Vision corridors into the project have been carefully studied from the freeway and major streets, inviting all to use this unique and convenient urban centre. Included within the project is a Community Center constructed and dedicated as a public facility for city use.

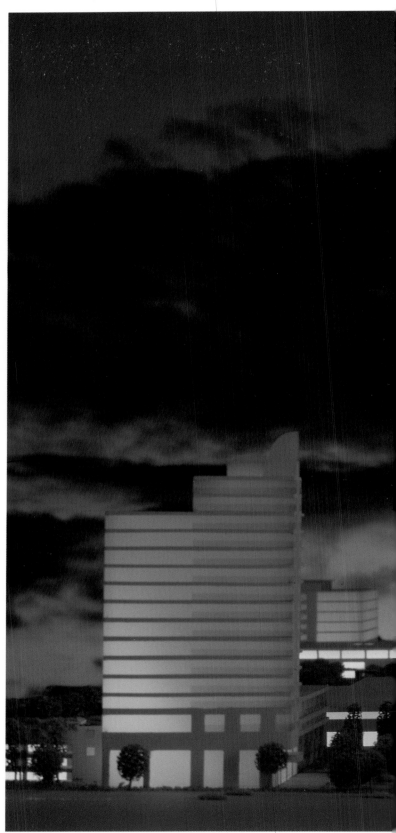

Kings Hill

LOCATION: West Malling, Kent, England

SIZE: 650 acres

FUNCTION OF BUILDING: Speculative business development

DATE OF COMPLETION: Ongoing

MASTER PLANNER: Terence O'Rourke plc, Bournemouth, Dorset, England

The Kings Hill development will include commercial space, retail areas, housing, hotel and conference facilities and a university campus. The developers, Rouse Kent, represent the new convergence of private enterprise (the American company Rouse Associates) and the public purse (the University of Kent).

Rouse Kent envisage that Kings Hill will, when finished, share the ambience and corporate identity of Rouse Associates existing developments in the USA, such as this one in Florida.

Efficient traffic circulation is essential to a successful development and, as at Kings Hill, roads and roundabouts are the first elements to be completed.

Napa Valley Corporate Park

LOCATION: Napa Valley, California

NAME OF PROJECT: Napa Valley Corporate Park

SIZE: 1,000,000m²

FUNCTION OF BUILDING: Mixed use

DATE OF COMPLETION: Ongoing

ARCHITECT: Leason Pomeroy Associates, Irvine, California, USA

Napa Valley Corporate Park is a mixed-use office, hotel and R&D complex located in Napa, California. The 250-acre development was master planned by Leason Pomeroy Associates to serve as a guide for future projects within the park. LPA formulated into the design guidelines building locations, densities, accesses and materials.

A system of architectural walls has been incorporated into the guidelines as the unifying element. This system of walls announces pedestrian circulation, user signage, or service screening. These walls will be of different colours and textures but will be controlled overall by the design guidelines. To further ensure design conformity and compatibility of future buildings, architectural materials, colours and finishes are governed by the design guidelines.

Focus Business Service Centre

LOCATION: Berlin, Germany

NAME OF PROJECT: Focus Business Centre

FUNCTION OF BUILDING: Business administration office

DATE OF COMPLETION: 1990

ARCHITECT: J. Ganz and W. Rolfes, Berlin, Germany

Two large monolithic landmark buildings create a formal urban gateway to the Focus Business centre in Berlin.

As an example of a single cell business park, the complex comprises a cladding and glazing system of tripartite grids that organize the scale and composition of a large, but well-defined, modular system of urban tectonics.

Bristol-Myers Pharmaceutical Research Facility

NAME OF PROJECT: Bristol-Myers Pharmaceutical Research Center

SIZE: 90,000m^2

FUNCTION OF BUILDING: World headquarters building

DATE OF COMPLETION: 1986

ARCHITECT: The Stubbins Associates, Inc., Cambridge, Massachusetts, USA

Overall plans for the Pharmaceutical Research Center call for the construction of four buildings in a multi-phased programme. Situated on 177 acres in central Connecticut, the site development plan takes advantage of the natural beauty of the countryside, while being sensitive to the existing environment.

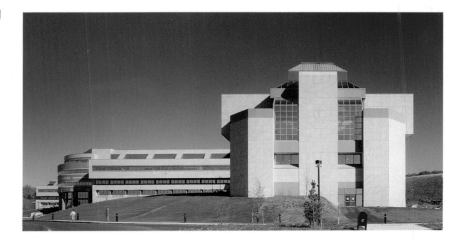

Carnegie Center

LOCATION: Princeton, New Jersey, USA

SIZE: 560 acres

DATE OF COMPLETION: 1998 (approximately 75%
completed 1990)

ARCHITECT: The Stubbins Associates, Inc., Cambridge,
Massachusetts, USA

Carnegie Center signals a vibrant, new approach to the
planning of a large-scale corporate community. Rational
use of the land, respect for the environment and
sensitivity to the needs of the suburban workers who use
it are the guiding principles behind the phased
development of the 520-acre site in Princeton, New
Jersey. Unique to Carnegie Center is the Greenway, a
linear, 20-acre common open area that forms the
pedestrian and recreational central spine of the office,
research and hotel complex. This concept facilitates
orientation within the large development and provides
attractive window views. Wide walkways link the
buildings lining this space, encouraging social interaction
and pedestrian movement through the active landscape.
Recreational amenities, jogging and bicycle paths bring
people together in public areas; paved roads and parking
areas located around the periphery of the complex limit
automobile use within this pedestrian-oriented
environment. Areas of water are designed to enhance
the landscape as well as function as retention basins.

The site, which consisted primarily of open fields, was
formerly used to cultivate sod. Sixty acres of wooded
area are part of the township's Greenbelt and will be
preserved as a wildlife sanctuary undisturbed by
development.

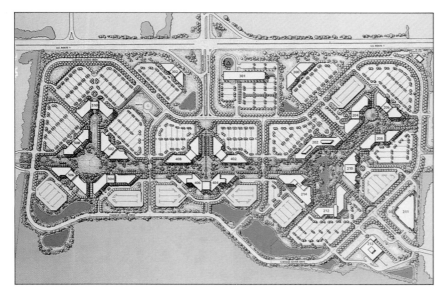

Giralda Farms

LOCATION: Madison and Chatham, New Jersey, USA

NAME OF PROJECT: Atlantic Mutual Administrative Center

SIZE: 48,000m²

FUNCTION OF BUILDING: Office space for marine insurance company

ARCHITECT: The Stubbins Associates, Inc., Cambridge, Massachusetts, USA

The Stubbins Associates served as Master Planners for the 130-acre Chatham parcel of the 310-acre former Geraldine Rockefeller-Dodge estate, and have designed three buildings for the Madison portion. Two completed projects in this portion include the four-storey Atlantic Mutual Administration Center and the North American Headquarters for Maersk Inc.

The Atlantic Mutual project is sited to take advantage of the verdant natural land forms and mature trees of Giralda Farms. A 1.5 acre reflecting pond forms a central feature and dramatically highlights the building from the entrance driveway. A four-storey atrium at the building's centre faces the pond at entry level and offers additional views of distant hills from its upper landings.

Exterior materials of granite and glass harmonize with the landscape and give a dignified character appropriate to one of the country's oldest marine insurance companies.

Giralda Farms continued over page

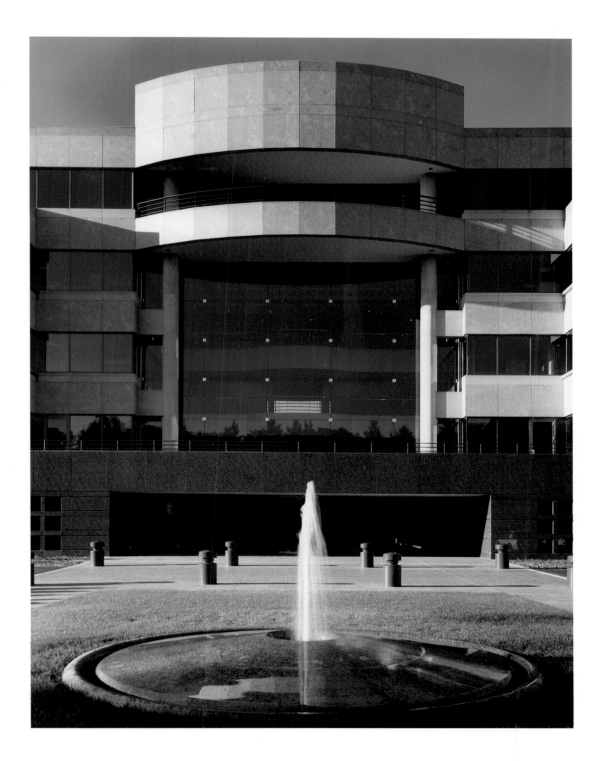

Atlantic Mutual Administration Center

King Street Station

LOCATION: Alexandria, Virginia, USA

SIZE: 314,000m^2

FUNCTION OF BUILDING: Office, hotel and retail development

DATE OF COMPLETION: Ongoing

MASTER PLAN: Keyes Condon Florance Eichbaum Esocoff King Architects, Washington DC, USA

The project is located at King Street Metro Station on a 7-acre site. The resulting plan is organized around generously landscaped plazas and walkways which encourage pedestrian use. A large crescent-shaped plaza is formed by the 260-room hotel and flanking office structures, with a retail pavilion.

Nynex

LOCATION: Orangetown, New York, USA

NAME OF PROJECT: Nynex Mobile Communications HQ

SIZE: 22,000m²

FUNCTION OF BUILDING: Offices

DATE OF COMPLETION: 1990

ARCHITECT: Hellmuth, Obata & Kassabaum, Inc.,
St Louis, Missouri, USA.

The Nynex project is sited within an existing corporate
park, also master-planned by Hellmuth, Obata &
Kassabaum.

Solana

LOCATION: Dallas/Fort Worth, Texas, USA

SIZE: 850 acres

DATE OF COMPLETION: Ongoing

ARCHITECT: Leason Pomeroy Associates, Irvine, California, USA

More than two million square meters of commercial development is planned on this 850-acre site. The mixed-use business community will be built in three phases over 10 years. The initial phase will establish the heart and character of the project. It includes office space and support facilities for IBM, the Village Center, a fitness sports club, a luxury hotel, 100,000m^2 office space and a 130,000m^2 national marketing center for IBM.

Other elements of the plan will be added as individual 'haciendas' along the internal circulation fitting into open clearings while preserving the natural forested areas.

The IBM Marketing Facility was designed by Ricardo Legoreta in association with LPA. A major water feature connects the building to a water element as part of a uniquely designed urban freeway connection. This urban design spans the freeway linking both sides of the Westlake and Southlake developments.

Solana continued over page

Solana continued

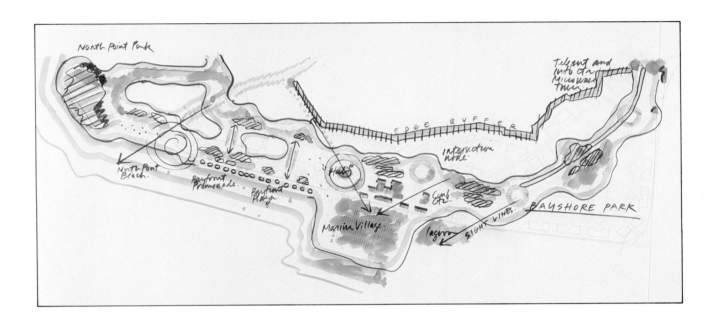

Harbor Bay

LOCATION: Alameda, California, USA

SIZE: 425 acres

DATE OF COMPLETION: Ongoing

ARCHITECT: Leason Pomeroy Associates, Irvine, California, USA

The park theme centres around its most spectacular amenity: the San Francisco Bay. Extensions of existing waterways, in the form of ponds, lagoons, and lakes, become focal points around which the major activity centres are clustered.

The Park Idea: Variations on a Theme

The philological association between the words *park* and *paradise*, and the biblical concept of paradise as an ideal or idealized place, have stimulated artists to construct romantic images of the park as a place for resting, eating, conversation, love and play.

The natural, royal and cosmopolitan parks of eighteenth-century London harnessed this Persian-Arcadian idea of the park as an irrigated haven for trees, shrubs and wildlife to be enjoyed on horseback, or via *la promenade*.

The brick walls of the early Persian parks have been replaced by the façades of city buildings, leaving gardens like Manhattan's Central Park as vital urban lungs breathing fresh air into the lives of a *cosmopolitia* eager for exercise and relaxation. The quality of the urban park is that it is discrete from the city, although part of its structural matrix. The frailty is that the park, as always, will suffer from a lack of security, with violence, rape and robbery becoming commonplace amongst the shadows of urban woodlands.

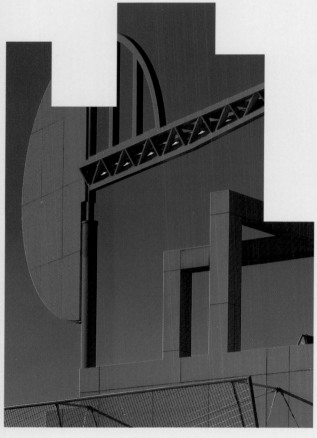

By moving the park *idea* away from the city centre, to a place accessible only by car, and laying over this concept the corporate office as a concrete policeman, it would seem that a new paradise might be made. At least, this is the philosophy of the third and fourth generation business park builders. But as art and science join suit with commerce to rub shoulders with safari parks, marine parks, national parks and adventure parks, one is left to wonder whether there will be anything left in the city for those who cannot afford to leave.

Park Central

LOCATION: Dallas, Texas, USA

NAME OF PROJECT: Four Forest Plaza

SIZE: 105,000m^2

FUNCTION OF BUILDING: Office

DATE OF COMPLETION: 1986

ARCHITECT: Hardy McCullah/MCM Architects Inc.,
Dallas, Texas, USA

If there has been an orthodoxy established in the design
of business parks worldwide, it is that they are generally
in suburban or semi-rural locations demanding a
relatively low-rise construction. High-rise buildings have
been traditionally located downtown, forming a cluster
of landmarks that establish the commercial matrix of the
city to which they belong. The Park Central Business
Campus located at North Dallas's major crossroads
between North Central Expressway and the LBJ Freeway
shifts this traditonal centre of gravity by building a high-
rise business park in a traditionally low-rise
neighbourhood. Four Forest Plaza is a nineteen-storey
tower in the Park that forms part of a fourth generation
business community which includes entertainment,
hotels, athletic clubs, medical and child-care facilities, a
post office and a Dallas Area Rapid Transport station.

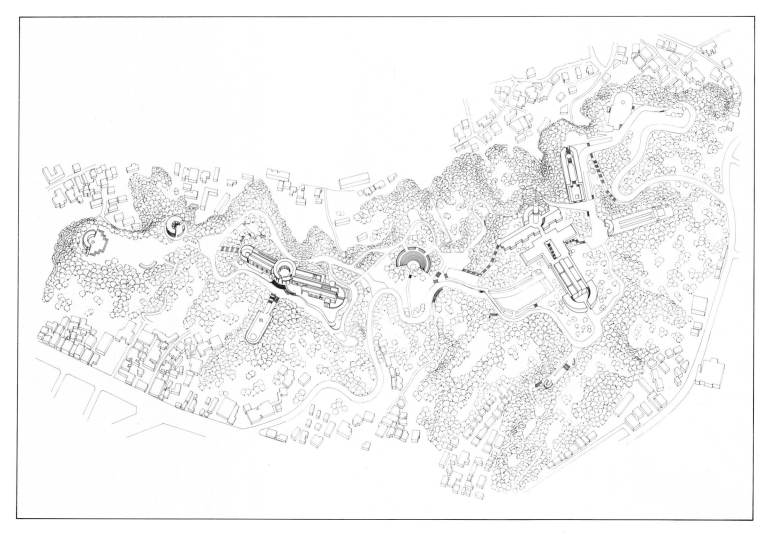

Hijiyama Art Park

LOCATION: Hiroshima, Japan

NAME OF PROJECT: Hiroshima City Museum of Contemporary Art

SIZE: 3,709.93m²

FUNCTION OF BUILDING: Art Museum

DATE OF COMPLETION: 1988

ARCHITECT: Kisho Kurakawa Architect, Tokyo, Japan

The site, on top of a 50-metre-high hill, was also master-planned by Kurokawa. The hill itself bears resemblence to the Acropolis in Athens and there are also plans for a museum and library besides the art museums. The whole is surrounded by the greenery of a nearby primeval forest and completely shut off from the noise of the city. There are pedestrian paths completely divorced from automobile areas, and attached to the art and cultural facilities, a sculpture park, outdoor school, vistas, open areas and nature walks.

Hijiyama Art Park continued over page

210

Hijiyama Art Park continued

The museum is large by Japanese standards. In consideration of the view from the city, 60 per cent has been put below ground. As the building becomes, in effect, the roof of the site, it exceeds 660 feet in length. To facilitate circulation, there are many staircases which by plan are placed redundantly to create a more artistic space.

The whole building effectively employs the axes created by its relation to other facilities, which are all tied together in the approach plaza in the centre of the building. And, with so much of the building below ground, the earth has been shifted from the sides of the building in places and large openings placed in the outside in the lower levels to mitigate the sunken effect on visitors.

The design of the roof and the wall of this building was metaphorically introduced from the traditional nineteenth-century warehouse, the 'kura'. As for the materials of the façade, stones, tiles, and aluminium are used all together, effectively creating the additional atmosphere of the future to the traditional elements.

Yachimun

LOCATION: Nakakami, Okinawa Province, Japan

SIZE: 39,600m²

FUNCTION OF BUILDING: Ceramicists' Village

DATE OF COMPLETION: 1980

ARCHITECT: Takumi Architects and Engineers

Historically, the island of Okinawa has always been a centre for ceramics. This village was purpose-built to promote regional development and at the same time preserve and develop the traditions and techniques of ceramics. The word *Yamichun* is a Ryukuan dialect word for ancient ceramics. Sited on land reclaimed after an American military base was decommissioned, the village is built mainly from recycled materials – salvaged red roof tiles and discarded telephone poles. This makes for low-cost, sturdy buildings that suit the setting and the nature of the village's function.

The settlement of ceramics workshops and modest living accommodation shelters under low pantile roofs built on timber frames and indigenous dry-stone walling. Fuel for the kilns is stored under a low shed that walks up a hillside to poke its nose at the outside world.

Cité des Sciences et de l'Industrie

LOCATION: Paris, France

FUNCTION OF BUILDING: Science and technology museum

ARCHITECT: Bernard Tschumi, Paris, France

The park at La Villette could be said to be dedicated to science, culture and leisure. The architect and master planner, Bernard Tschumi, not only solved the pragmatics of eating, walking, talking and learning but settled them within a planning matrix that, at certain nodal points, gives rise to a number of follies that have been critically considered as architectonic paradigms to the philosphy of deconstructionism that is normally associated with literary critical theory. So it could be said that the park is a park of culture, in that its very being is a physical demonstration of an intellectual activity and collaboration between an architectural theorist and the philosopher Jacques Derrida.

Cite des Sciences et de l'Industrie continued over page

Cite des Sciences et de l'Industrie continued

Although the follies have a conventional function, housing such Parisienne institutions as the café, they also stand as objects for study and contemplation by their role as architectonic paradigms to the complex and sometimes contradictory intellectual position embodied within the theories of deconstruction, which necessarily argue that the space *between* each of the follies is as relevant a subject for philosophising as is the object itself.

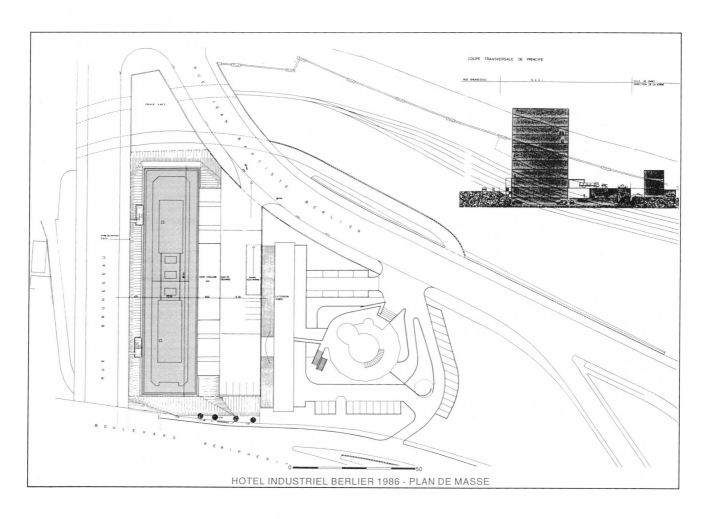

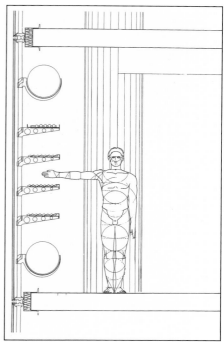

HOTEL INDUSTRIEL BERLIER 1986 - PLAN DE MASSE

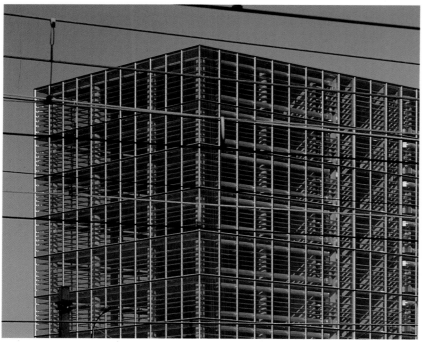

Hotel Industriel Berlier

LOCATION: Paris, France

NAME OF PROJECT: Hotel Industriel Berlier

SIZE: 10,000m²

FUNCTION OF BUILDING: Speculative industrial building

DATE OF COMPLETION: 1990

ARCHITECT: Dominique Perrault, Architecte, Paris, France

Dominique Perrault was commissioned to design a multi-level building in the form of a slatted business park, rising ten floors above an underground car park. Each deck provides clear space for occupation by business and/or light industrial or research activities, forming a high rise business park. The uniformity of function provides for an anonymity of architectural expression that is simultaneously foreboding and engaging.

Index of Projects

A

Antrim Technology Park, Antrim, Northern Ireland 84–7
Arlington Business Park, Theale, Reading, Berkshire, England 76–7
Auckland Business Park, Milton Keynes, Bedfordshire, England 56–7
Aztec West, Almondsbury, Bristol, Avon, England 134–153

B

Hotel Berlier, Paris, France 220–1
Birmingham Business Park, Solihull, Warwickshire, England 158–161
Bishops Square, Hatfield Business Park, Hatfield, Hertfordshire, England 38–9
Blackbrook, Taunton, Somerset, England 58–9
Bricklayers Arms, London, England 64–7
Bristol Myers Pharmaceutical Research Facility, Wallingford, Connecticut, USA 190-1
Burbank Gateway Center, Burbank, California, USA 182–3

C

Callendar Business Park, Falkirk, Scotland 45–7
Carnegie Center, Princeton, New Jersey, USA 192–3
Capability Green, Luton Hoo, Luton, Bedfordshire, England 102–5
Centre Park, Warrington, Cheshire, England 60–1
Chester Business Park, Chester, Cheshire, England 43–4
Chilworth Research Centre, Chilworth, Southampton, Hampshire, England 32–5
Chiswick Park, London, England 94–9
Cité des Sciences et de l'Industrie, Parc de la Villette, Paris, France 216–19
Cody Business Park, London, England 52–3
County Oak, Crawley, West Sussex, England 54–5

D

Dundee Technology Park, Dundee, Scotland 50–1

E

Eden Park, Fenstanton, Cambridgeshire, England 90–91
Edinburgh Business Park, Edinburgh, Scotland 174–5

F

Focus Business Centre, Berlin, Germany 188–9

G

Giralda Farms, Madison and Chatham, New Jersey, USA 194–7
Greenway Business Park, Richardson, Texas, USA 168–171

H

Harbor Bay, Alameda, California, USA 205
Hampshire Corporate Park, Chandlers Ford, Hampshire, England 40–2
Hayward Business Park, Havant, Hampshire, England 37
Hijiyama Art Park, Hiroshima, Japan 210–13
Hotel Berlier, Paris, France 220–21

I

Irvine Freeway Spectrum, Irvine, California, USA 82–3

K

Kettering Venture Park, Kettering, Northamptonshire, England 176–7
Kings Mill, West Malling, Kent, England 184–5
King Street Station, Alexandria, Virginia, USA 198–9

L

Landmark Square, Tempe, Arizona, USA 132–3
Letchworth Business Park, Letchworth, Hertfordshire, England 62–3

M

Macarthur Place, Santa Ana, California, USA 180–1
Marina Village, Alameda, California, USA 172–3

N

Napa Valley Corporate Park, Napa Valley, California, USA 186–7
New Square, Bedfont Lakes, Feltham, Middlesex, England 90–3
Newbury Business Park, Newbury, Berkshire, England 72–5
Nynex, Orangetown, New York, USA 200–1

P

Park Central, Dallas, Texas, USA 208–9
Parque Tecnologico del Valles, Cerdanyola, Barcelona, Spain 156–7
Peel Park, East Kilbride, Lanarkshire, Scotland 48–9

S

Sanden International, Wylie, Texas, USA 178–9
Sintra Business Park, Sintra, Lisbon, Portugal 154–5
South Newmoor, Irvine, Ayrshire, Scotland 28–9
Solana, Dallas/Fort Worth, Texas, USA 202–4
Solent Business Park, Fareham, Hampshire, England 162–5
Stockley Park, Heathrow, London, England 106–127

T

Thames Valley Business Park, Reading, Berkshire, England 68–9
Tri City Landing, San Bernardino, California, USA 130–1
Tulips, Hampshire Corporate Park, Chineham, Basingstoke, Hampshire, England 30–1

V

Valley View, Commerce Center, Santa Fe Springs, California, USA 80–1
Vintage Park, Foster City, California, USA 128–9
Vision Park, Histon, Cambridgeshire, England 78–9

W

Waterside Business Park, Witham, Essex, England 36

Y

Yakimun Ceramicist's Village, Yakimun, Okinawa, Japan 214–15

Directory of Practising Architects

This directory lists the addresses of architects in current practice. While every effort has been made to ensure that this list was correct at the time of going to press, subsequent changes in address or status are beyond the publishers' remit.

Ahrends, Burton and Koralek
Unit 1, 7 Chalcot Road, London NW1 8LH, England
PROJECT: ABK building, Chiswick Park 98–9

Arup Associates
37 Fitzroy Square, London NW1P 5NA, England
PROJECTS: Landscape Master Plan, The Arena, 1 Long Walk Road, 3 Long Walk Road, 4 Roundwood Avenue: all at Stockley Park 108–125

Atkins Lister Drew
Woodcote Drive, Ashley Road, Kettering KT18 5DW, Northamptonshire, England
PROJECT: RCI Building, Kettering Venture Park 176–7

Auckett Associates
123 Chelsea Embankment, London SW3 4LA, England
PROJECTS: Master Plan, Birmingham Business Park 158–9; Master Plan, Solent Business Park 162–3

Beardsmore Associates
22–54 Prince of Wales Road, London NW5 3LG, England
PROJECT: Arena Restaurant, Stockley Park 116–7

Broadway Malyan
Osprey House, Station Road, Addlestone KT15 2BH, Surrey, England
PROJECTS: Sintra Business Park 154–5; Thames Valley Business Park 68–9

Cristian Cirici & Associats
C/Caspe 151, 0908013 Barcelona, Spain
PROJECT: Parque Tecnologico del Valles 156–7

Edward Cullinan Architects
The Wharf, Baldwin Terrace, London N1 7RU, England
PROJECTS: Chilworth Research Centre 32–5; New Square 90–3

CZWG Architects
17 Bowling Green Lane, London EC1R 0BD, England
PROJECT: 200 Aztec West 148–151

DY Davies Associates
1 Church Terrace, Richmond TW10 6SE, Surrey, England
PROJECT: Letchworth Business Park 62–3

ERP Architects Ltd
21 Douglas Street, London SW1P 4PG, England
PROJECT: Inmos Building, Aztec West 137

Terry Farrell & Partners
The Old Aero Works, 17 Hatton Street, London NW8 8PL, England
PROJECT: Master Plan, Chiswick Park 94–5

Fitzroy Robinson Parnership
77 Portland Place, London W1N 4EP, England
PROJECT: Arlington Business Park 76–7

Peter Foggo Associates
55 Charterhouse Street, London EC1M 6HA, England
PROJECTS: Peter Foggo Associates building, Stockley Park 126–7; Peter Foggo Associates building, Chiswick Park 98–9

Foster Associates
Riverside 3, Albert Wharf, 22 Hester Road, London SW11 4AN, England
PROJECTS: Foster Associates building, Chiswick Park 96–7

Bruce Gilbreth Architects
100 Oxford Street, London W1N 9FB, England
PROJECT: Capability Green 102–5

HGP Greentree Allchurch Evans Ltd
110 Wickham Road, Fareham, Hampshire, England
PROJECT: Hampshire Corporate Park 40–2

Hellmuth, Obata + Kassabaum Inc
1831 Chestnut Street, St Louis, Missouri 63103–2231, USA
PROJECT: Nynex 200–1

Michael Hopkins & Partners
27 Broadley Street, London NW1 6LG, England
PROJECT: New Square 90–3

Department of Architecture/Irvine Development Corporation, Irvine, Ayrshire, Scotland
PROJECT: South Newmoor 28–9

Jestico + Whiles
14 Stephenson Way, London NW1 2HD, England
PROJECT: Callendar Park 45–7

Kennedy FitzGerald Associates
3 Eglantine Place, Belfast BT9 6EY, N. Ireland
PROJECT: Antrim Technology Park 84–7

Keyes Condon Florance Eichbaum Esocoff King
1100 New York Avenue NW, Suite 400 East Tower, Washington DC 2000 S, USA
PROJECT: King Street Station 198–9

Kisho Kurakawa Architect & Associates
Aoyama Building 11F, 1-2-3 Kita Aoyama, Minato-ku, Tokyo, Japan
PROJECT: Hijiyama Art Park 210–13

Leason Pomeroy Associates
One Venture, Suite 300, Irvine, California 92718, USA
PROJECTS: Burbank Gateway Center 192–3; Irvine Freeway Spectrum 82–3; Landmark Square 132–3; Macarthur Place 180–1; Marina Village 172–3; Napa Valley Corporate Park 186–7; Solana 202–4; Tri City Landing 130–1; Valley View 80–1; Vintage Park 128–9

John Lyall Architects
Bridge Studios, 107a Hammersmith Bridge Road, London W6 9DA, England
PROJECT: Tulips 30–1

Mason Richards Partnership
Salisbury House, Tettenhall Road, Wolverhampton WV1 4SG, England
PROJECT: Master Plan, Kettering Venture Park, 176–7

Hardy McCullah/MLM Architects
12221 Merit Drive, Suite 280, Dallas, Texas 75251, USA
PROJECTS: Greenway Business Park 168–71; Park Central 208–9; Sanden International 178–9

Richard Meier Associates
475 10th Avenue, New York, New York 10018, USA
PROJECT: Master Plan, Edinburgh Park 174–5

Nicoll Russell
Westfield Road, Broughty Ferry, Dundee DD5 1ED, Scotland
PROJECT: Dundee Technology Park 50–1

ORMS
1 Pine Street, London EC1R 0JH, England
PROJECTS: Blackbrook 58–9; Centre Park 60–1

Ormrod & Partners
49 Rodney Street, Liverpool L11 9EP, England
PROJECT: Chester Business Park 43–4

Terence O'Rourke Plc
Everdene House, Wessex Fields, Deansleigh Road, Bournemouth, Hampshire, England BH7 7DU
PROJECT: Master Plan, Kings Hill 184–5

Eric Parry Associates
3 Stukeley Street, London WC2B, England
PROJECT: Eric Parry Associates building, Stockley Park 124–5

Dominic Perrault Associates
26–34 rue Bruneseau, 785013 Paris, France
PROJECT: Hotel Berlier 220–1

Ian Ritchie Architect
0 Building, Metropolitan Wharf, Wapping Wall, London E1 9SS, England
PROJECT: 3 Furzeground Way, Stockley Park 126–7

Richard Rogers Partnership
Thames Wharf, Rainville Road, London W5 9HA, England
PROJECT: Richard Rogers Partnership building, Stockley Park 124–5

Sansome Hall
Regency Court, 220 Upper Fifth Street, Milton Keynes MK9 2HR, Bedfordshire, England
PROJECT: Auckland Park 56–7

Scott Brownrigg + Turner
Bradstone Brook, Shalford, Guildford, Surrey GU8 8HT, England
PROJECT: Bishops Square 38–9

The Stubbins Associates
1033 Massachusetts Avenue, Cambridge, Massachusetts 02138, USA
PROJECTS: Bristol-Myers Pharmaceutical Research Facility 190–1; Carnegie Center 192–3; Giralda Farms 194–7

Brian Taggart Associates
now Cassidy Taggart Partnership
7 Netherwood Road, London W14, England
PROJECT: Digital building, Aztec West 147

Tartan Tectonics
Bridge House, Bridge Street, Cambridge, England
PROJECTS: Eden Park 88–9; Vision Park 78–9

Robert Tear Architects
Quayside House, Central Road, Eastern Docks, Southampton SO1 1AH, Hampshire, England
PROJECTS: Hayward Business Park 37; Waterside Business Park 36

Thorpe Architecture
Sparks Yard, Tarrant Street, Arundel BN18 93B, West Sussex, England
PROJECTS: Master Plan, Aztec Centre 134–5; Midland Bank, Aztec Centre 141–4; Cody Business Park 52–3; County Oak 54–5; Master Plan, Newbury Business Park 72–5; Parkside, Birmingham Business Park 160–1; Solent Centre 1641–5

Troughton McAslan
202 Kensington Church Street, London W8 4BP, England
PROJECT: 6 Roundwood Avenue, Stockley Park 114–5

Vincent and Gorbing
Sterling Court, Norton Road, Stevenage SG1 1JY, Hertfordshire, England
PROJECT: McDonnell Douglas building, Aztec West 152–3

Photographic Acknowledgements

8/9 **Dawson Strange/Arlington Properties**; 10/11/12/13 **Stanhope Properties**; 14 **The Stubbins Associates**; 14 **Dawson Strange/Arlington Properties**; 15 **Steven Whittaker/LPA**; 17 **Peter Cook/Beardsmore Associates**; 18/19 **RIBA**; 20/1 **Dawson Strange/Arlington Properties**; 22/3 **Thorpe Architecture**; 24/5 **Dawson Strange/Arlington Properties**; 26L **Keith Gibson**; 26R **Jo Peck & John Reid/Alaska Davies**; 27L **Alastair Hunter**; 27R **Edward Cullinan Architects**; 28/9 **Keith Gibson**; 30/1 **John Lyall Architects**; 32/3 **Edward Cullinan Architects**; 34/5 **Edward Cullinan Architects**; 36/7 **David Williams/Robert Tear Architects**; 38/9 **Dawson Strange/Arlington Properties**; 40/2 **Joe Lowe**; 43/4 **John Mills Photography**; 45/6/7 **Alastair Hunter**; 48/9 **Graham Lees**; 50/1 **Alastair Hunter**; 52/3/4/5 **Thorpe Architecture**; 56/7 **Terrapin Ltd**; 58/9 **ORMS**; 60/1 **Paul White Photography, Wakefield**; 62/3 **British Steel Products/PRP**; 64/5/6/7 **Jo Peck & John Reid/Alaska Davies**; 68/9 **Roger D. Smith/Broadway Malyan**; 70L **Dawson Strange/Arlington Properties**; 70R **LPA**; 71L **Stanhope Properties**; 71R **LPA**; 72/3 **Dawson Strange/Arlington Properties**; 74/5 **Dawson Strange/Arlington Properties**; 76/7 **Fitzroy Robinson/Leighton Gibbins**; 78/9 **Astrawall**; 80/1 **Adrian Velicescu/LPA**; 82/3 **Timothy Hursley/LPA**; 84/5/6/7 **Kennedy FitzGerald**; 88/9 **Peter Mackinver/Arup Associates**; 90/1 **Denis Gilbert**; 92/3 **Michael Hopkins & Partners; The Building Magazine**; 94/5/6/7/8/9, 100/1 **Stanhope Properties**; 102/4 **Bruce Gilbreth**; 104/5 **PRP/British Steel Products**; 106/8/9/10/11 **Stanhope Properties**; 112 **Beardsmore Associates/drawing by Steve Tompkins**; 113 **Stanhope Properties**; 114T **Joe Lowe**; 114B **Stanhope Properties**; 115 **Peter Cook/Beardsmore Associates**; 116/17/18/19/20/21/22/23/24/25/26/27 **Stanhope Properties**; 128/29 **LPA**; 130/31 **LPA**; 132/33 **John Connell/LPA**; 134/35/36/37/38/39/40/41 **Dawson Strange/Arlington Properties**; 142/43 **Thorpe Architecture**; 144/45/46/47/48 **Dawson Strange/Arlington Properties**; 149/50/51 **CZWG**; 152/53 **Dawson Strange/Arlington Properties**; 154/55 **Nick Wright/Broadway Malyan**; 156/57 **Lluis Casals/Cristian Cirici & Associates**; 158/59 **Dawson Strange/Arlington Properties**; 160/61/62/63/64/65 **Dawson Strange/Arlington Properties**; 166L **Hardy McCullah/MLM Architects Inc**; 166R **Dawson Strange/Arlington Properties**; 167L **The Stubbins Associates**; 167R **Roy Wright/Hellmuth/Obata/Kassabaum**; 169/69 **Hardy McCullah/MLM Architects Inc**; 170/71 **Hardy McCullah/MLM Architects Inc**; 172/73 **Steve Whittaker**; 175 **Guthrie Photography**; 176/77 **Dawson Strange/Arlington Properties**; 178/79 **Hardy McCullah/MLM Architects Inc**; 180/81 **Adrian Velicescu/LPA**; 182/83 **Mike Sasso/LPA**; 184/85 **Rouse Kent**; 186/87 **John Connell/LPA**; 188/89 **Architectural Association**; 190/91 **Nick Wheeler/Wheeler Photographic/The Stubbins Associates**; 192/93/94/95 **The Stubbins Associates**; 198/99 **Keyes/Condon/Florance/Eichbaum/Esocoff/King**; 200/1 **Roy Wright/Hellmuth/Obata/Kassabaum**; 202/3 **Hedrich Blessing/LPA**; 204 **Hedrich Blessing/LPA**; 205 **Ronald Moore/LPA**; 206L **Michel Denancé**; 206R **Richard Bryant/Arcaid**; 207L **Tomio Ohashi**; 207R **Tomio Ohashi**; 208/209 **Hardy McCullah/MLM Architects Inc**; 210/211 **Tomio Ohashi**; 212/13 **Tomio Ohashi**; 214/15 **The Japan Architect**; 216/17 **Richard Bryant/Arcaid**; 218/19 **Richard Bryant/Arcaid**; 220/21 **Michel Denancé**